Plea
Colle
124
Ham
East

GW01144006

A PLAY BY TOM BECKER

UNTIL THE LAST LIGHT FADES

Activities by
Wendy Costin

ALWAYS LEARNING **PEARSON**

Published by Pearson Education Limited, Edinburgh Gate, Harlow, Essex, CM20 2JE.

www.pearsonschoolsandfecolleges.co.uk

Play text © Tom Becker 2013
Typeset by Phoenix Photosetting, Chatham, Kent, UK
Cover photo/illustration © Pearson Education Limited
Activities text © Pearson Education Limited 2013

The right of Tom Becker to be identified as author of this work has been asserted by him in accordance with the Copyright, Designs and Patents Act 1988.

First published 2013

16 15 14 13
11 10 9 8 7 6 5 4 3 2 1

British Library Cataloguing in Publication Data
A catalogue record for this book is available from the British Library

ISBN 9780435149437

CAUTION
All rights whatsoever in this play are strictly reserved. Requests to reproduce the text in whole or in part should be addressed to the publisher.

Copyright notice
All rights reserved. No part of this publication may be reproduced in any form or by any means (including photocopying or storing it in any medium by electronic means and whether or not transiently or incidentally to some other use of this publication) without the written permission of the copyright owner, except in accordance with the provisions of the Copyright, Designs and Patents Act 1988 or under the terms of a licence issued by the Copyright Licensing Agency, Saffron House, 6–10 Kirby Street, London EC1N 8TS (www.cla.co.uk). Applications for the copyright owner's written permission should be addressed to the publisher.

Printed and bound in China (CTPS/01)

Contents

Introduction v
Cast list vii
Staging suggestions ix
The Play 1
Glossary 84
Activities 86

Introduction

Experience has taught me to keep track of my ideas, as readers are often curious about where they come from. I only wish I could give them better answers. *Until The Last Light Fades* began with me watching a television programme featuring a lighthouse, and thinking that it was a naturally dramatic building – and potentially a great setting for a story. Looking back through my notebook, I found this initial tentative suggestion:

'A girl tends a lighthouse on her own. No parents. Waiting for someone? Not helping ships but wrecking them?'

I never know exactly where I'm going with an idea at first – but I remember having a very clear image of a girl walking down the spiral staircase of a lighthouse, with a sense of some unseen danger in the shadows. That's usually a good sign, as it suggests I've got a sense of both location and atmosphere in my head.

When the opportunity arose to write a play, it seemed natural to develop that image and begin to build a world around it. A good friend of mine gave me a compilation CD with a track called *Lost Coastlines* by Okkervil River – I think I misinterpreted the lyrics but it got me thinking about a drowning world, and was often playing in the background as I was writing. Precious pebbles of inspiration dot the shores of our everyday lives; part of the job of writing is to pick them up, brush the sand off them and put them somewhere safe. You might not need them immediately, but one day you'll be glad they're there.

Cast list

Luke, a Junior Ship Clerk in the Ocean Commission
Elle, the Keeper of the lighthouse
Sloop, Elle's assistant
Rowetta, the landlady of The Anchor
Pool, a dredgerman and regular at The Anchor
Fluke, a fisherman and regular at The Anchor
Bailey, the Wharfinger
Sophie, his wife
Wanda, Luke's friend on Pharos
Ripley, a Senior Ship Clerk in the Ocean Commission
Audrey, a Flotsam girl
Stranger/The Examiner
Forecaster on the wireless
Assorted **Crewmembers**

Staging suggestions

The way that any director or cast approaches staging a play is bound to be only one way of looking at the text. Even the oldest plays are endlessly reinterpreted as we continue to find new ways of looking at them. Quite simply, there is no right or wrong way to stage a piece, but there are ways which offer greater or lesser challenges to actors and audiences. These staging suggestions will depend more on developing a strong ensemble feel within your cast than they will on bulky and costly sets. As a theatre-goer, I feel the drama starts to die the moment a curtain closes and we hear the scenery trundling around, and it can take a long time to regain lost momentum. I always want the story and the characters to keep moving. I think audiences are happy to suspend disbelief and use their own imaginations if you reward them with a performance that has wit, charm, style and vision, even if you are working in a limited or limiting space.

Until The Last Light Fades is a strange and complex play. It is set in a world we feel we know in some ways but in others it is unlike anything we have experienced. It is almost a parallel world, an unnerving world, a dark and elemental world. It is no coincidence that the title mentions light, the action revolves around a lighthouse and a central character lives in a world of darkness. The whole piece is about revealing and hiding, about secrecy and openness, the final image is of people looking into a bright sun, protecting their eyes – Tom Becker's writing gives us important clues for direction, design and performance style.

Locations
The Locations needed to tell this story are as follows:

- The Anchor Pub
- A lighthouse (the top and bottom of it!)
- The Sea at Night

- A Sea Wall
- A Clerk's Office
- The Deck of a Dredger

Costumes

I found the films of Terry Gilliam and Jean-Pierre Jeunet coming to mind when I read this text. It may be that their visual vocabulary has something to offer us here. The Gilliam/Jeunet world often feels historical and futuristic at the same time and this can help set an interesting and distinctive tone. Nothing in this piece should feel *quite right;* consider using clothes that are too big or small for the actors, perhaps use a distinctive colour palette or unusual props to make things feel recognisable but odd.

Light and Sound

Light is at the heart of this piece; it is a theme and a motif which should not be used casually. Unusually for a theatre-piece, I suggest you treat *darkness* as your starting point and only reveal what you need to. Never flood the performance area with light until the end which offers some respite and some sense of redemption. Perhaps light each place discreetly and sparsely. A few bare bulbs hanging over a table or two will make The Anchor feel (as Tom Becker intends) like it is hunkered down against the elements.

Similarly, never let the audience forget that they are watching the activities of an island, open to the sea and the seasons. Cries of gulls and the sound of the waves should never be far from their ears. If you can drag in some seaweed for that authentic salty aroma, then do so.

Transitions

This doesn't feel like a play which will benefit from gaps between scenes. If any do occur then build the sea sounds and the bird cries. Keep those watching on edge and alert. If there is scene-setting to be done, have the actors or scene-setters work in darkness with torches as if they were wreckers working at night.

Pay attention to how your event opens and closes. Try to do as much as possible to change the feel of your auditorium, netting, buoys and a pub sign swinging as the audience enters will all help to enhance the mood. If you have any pupils or teachers who are good at music-tech see if they can produce some soundtrack which fuses something historical (perhaps sea shanties) with something edgier & more contemporary, your pupils will be able to make pertinent and current suggestions.

Challenges

This play is peppered with challenges, some can be dealt with head on, others hinted at. The way I am suggesting you approach the staging of this piece will make the most of your cast, and will teach them a few things about contemporary performance, but you'll still need to think seriously about how to 'do the light'!

Scenes

The Anchor (scenes 1, 6)
Lighthouse (scenes 2, 4, 8, 10)
The Sea at Night (scene 3)
Sea Wall (scene 5, 11)
Clerk's Office (scene 7)
Dredger (scene 9)

Overview

This play is set on an island and I think that is a clue to successful staging. If you can stage this piece in the round at all, try to do so. That approach will make sense with this play more than most. Even if you have to put some of your audience on the stage to look down on the 'in the round' action, consider it. I think it will pay dividends.

I think the Lighthouse needs to dominate this piece so can be staged permanently and centrally. If this is built of scaffolding then we will have levels to look at (even if there are only two) and it will not obscure other scenes. Other scenes can even use the exterior of the light house to play against but they should never enter it. I suspect that with the exception of the sea wall, all the other settings (Clerks Office, Anchor, Dredger etc) can be temporary, can be placed and 'struck' very quickly. Be prepared to be very simplistic to help the audience know exactly where they are – have the 'Anchor' sign above all pub scenes and another for the Clerk's Office clearly visible during that portion of the drama.

Think in detail about how the scenes move from one into another. It might be nice if it felt like the set was 'swept in' and 'swept away' as if by the tides...for your actors to do this well will mean paying close attention to every detail about who does what and what goes where, but it will mean that every part of your event is watchable and memorable.

Drama boxes/cubes offer endless opportunities. If they have holes drilled to take rods with a rope attached then a dredge can easily be formed, seemingly from nowhere. One of the ropes or boxes can even have 'Dredger. Owner: Mr Pool, Registered: The Bluffs' on a sign attached to it.

Think of making the Clerk's Office look out-of-time. Perhaps Luke and Ripley could use Dickensian quills and laptops/tablets. This will add to the strangeness of the tone and remind us that we are somewhere strange and disconcerting.

It seems to me that there is no real way around having a large lamp, centre, on the lighthouse. It is a real beacon, a metaphor, a focal point, and the reason why Fluke falls to his death. Make sure that, when you construct the top of the lighthouse, there is enough space for all that action in the penultimate scene. Your actors will need space to perform and share their gestures and expressions with their audience.

The fall of Fluke is a moment which needs careful thought. Here is my suggestion; just as the actor playing Fluke is about to fall with his 'hoarse yell' you switch the audience's focus suddenly to somewhere else on stage – lights down on the Lighthouse and lights up on an actor in exactly the same costume as Fluke, standing up high (but not, vitally, as high as our 'real' Fluke). This actor continues the 'hoarse yell' and falls into the arms of the waiting cast below. These actors can even then seemingly wash

Fluke out to sea as he is lifelessly hoisted aloft onto their shoulders. Well rehearsed and cleanly executed, this should only take a few seconds, could be a memorable moment and will have dealt efficiently with a tricky stage direction. After the ersatz-Fluke is 'washed away' our focus falls back on the Lighthouse (where of course the actor playing Fluke has gone).

I hope these suggestions solve, rather than create, problems. They are intended to give your cast as much responsibility as possible. They aim to give your pupils a sense of the contemporary ensemble theatre-making which is widely used by companies like Complicité, Kneehigh and Improbable and will develop their performance skills rather than relying on expensive trickery.

Richard Conlon

For Lindsay

Scene 1

*The Bluffs is a remote island in a **turbulent** ocean, a tiny colony besieged by strange currents and unpredictable tides. A cluster of houses huddles around the base of a tall lighthouse like chilled travellers by a campfire. Night has fallen, bringing with it a violent, **goading** wind. Waves crash over The Bluffs' seawall, **sluicing** narrow streets with seawater and filling the air with spray. The lighthouse alone stands unbowed, a towering **sentinel** defiantly hurling light out over the dark ocean.*

*One of the buildings caught in the beam's path is The Anchor, whose windows periodically light up as a result. Despite its sturdy name, the inn's wooden rafters creak and groan in the buffeting winds like a ship **listing** upon the waves. Rowetta, the female captain of this decrepit, ale-soaked vessel, leans over the bar, staring disconsolately into space as regulars Fluke and Pool nurse their drinks. Eventually Rowetta straightens up and rings the brass bell above the bar.*

ROWETTA: Time at the bar, gentlemen! If you could finish your drinks, please. You may not want to go home, but I do.

POOL: Easy for you to say, Rowetta. You live upstairs. You don't have to go out into *that*. 5

Pool jerks his head in the direction of the howling gale outside.

ROWETTA: And how many paces is it exactly back to your house, Pool? Twenty? Thirty?

POOL: *(Grumpily)* I'm not saying it's *far*, as such. I'm just saying you shouldn't rush a man.

FLUKE: I'll be off soon, Rowetta, don't worry about that. Bit of splish and splash don't bother Fluke here. I spend so much time in the boat these days that the wife reckons I'm half-fish anyways.

POOL: *(Curiously)* Which half – top or bottom?

ROWETTA: Bottom, of course. It's his wife who's top-half fish.

POOL: Why do you think he spends so much time in the boat?

*As the other two crease up with laughter Fluke accepts their **jibes** with **benevolent** good humour.*

FLUKE: Now if you're saying there's something of the mermaid about my wife – even if she's upside down – I'll thank you for the compliment. Did I ever tell you about the time I fell in love with a real mermaid?

POOL: Only a few thousand times.

FLUKE: *(Wistfully)* Amazing creature she was, half of land and half of sea, **brine** sparkling in her hair. Most beautiful thing I ever saw.

POOL: A pretty pair you would have made.

FLUKE: But her feelings ebbed and flowed like the tide, and it wasn't long before her heart washed up on another shore … *(Brightly)* Still, there's no point **supping** on regret your whole life. I met my good lady wife a couple o' years later, and there was a happy ending after all.

SCENE 1

ROWETTA: And an even prettier pair you make.

FLUKE: Well, mock as you may, and say what you will, I have no complaints about my wife *or* the weather. Cod and haddock are welcome aboard my boat, and tuna and mackerel can wriggle in my net to their hearts' content, but I've no need for carp.

POOL: Hark at the philosopher fisherman!

FLUKE: I'll make no apologies and say no sorrys for my sunny outlook. As I always say to my good lady, we're the lucky ones.

ROWETTA: *(Incredulously)* The lucky ones? You've a funny idea of fortune, Fluke. There ain't much that's lucky about our situation.

FLUKE: I don't know. It could be worse.

ROWETTA: How, exactly? We're stuck on this godforsaken rock as it sinks beneath the waves, with little to occupy our minds but the wondering of what exactly will do for us in the end. Will we drown like our great-great grandfathers, or catch flood disease like our grandmothers? P'rhaps a bunch of Flotsam'll come ashore and murder us in our beds, or p'rhaps the well runs dry and we'll go brine drunk from swigging seawater. The only certainty is that what's left of our world is disappearing beneath our feet, and there's little chance of a happy ending, mermaids and good ladies notwithstanding.

And we're the lucky ones? Ha!

The men sip on their drinks, mulling over Rowetta's speech.

FLUKE: *(Nodding slowly)* That's one opinion, I s'pose. I've always been a 'glass half-full man', myself.

ROWETTA: You should be a 'glass completely empty man'. I'm not sitting here listening to you jabber on all night. 70

From outside a dog's bark carries on the whistling wind. Rowetta goes over to the window and peers into the darkness.

ROWETTA: Now what's got the Admiral in such a to-do …? Looks like someone on the path. It's a bit late for a visitor.

POOL: They must have come in on the oil barge. I heard it land a while back. 75

ROWETTA: Aye, you've got the sharpest ears on The Bluffs, except when it comes to me telling you to drink up. Shake a leg, will you?

The door to The Anchor crashes open, revealing a glimpse of a wild and windy landscape outside. Luke struggles inside the inn and closes the door behind him, panting heavily with the effort. The young man's hair is plastered to his forehead, and his clothes are wet through.

ROWETTA: *(Cheerily)* Still raining, is it? 80

*Struggling to regain his composure, Luke walks slowly over to the bar and sits down upon a stool, where he finds himself the subject of three **inquisitive** stares.*

LUKE: Good evening.

ROWETTA: Compliments of the season to you too, young man. What can I do for you? If it's a

	drink you're after, I'm afraid I've already called time.
LUKE:	That's all right, I've—
ROWETTA:	Might you be looking for a room for the night, then? The Anchor is known across the seas for its warm welcome.
LUKE:	No, I'm going to stay at the—
ROWETTA:	Then what do you want? You're not Flotsam, are you?

Luke shakes his head.

ROWETTA:	*(Firmly)* 'Cause a warm welcome to an honest traveller is one thing, but opening our doors to Flotsam quite another. The Bluffs is crowded enough as it is and getting smaller everyday, thank you very much. We don't need travelling folk washing up here with their charmed seaweed and nicking everything that's not nailed down. You can carry on to Greenland with the rest of them if that's your plan.
LUKE:	No ma'am, I'm—
ROWETTA:	Well *something* brought you here. This isn't the kind of place you just happen across. All this mystery is making me suspicious.
POOL:	It'd seem to me, Rowetta, that you might improve your chances of learning the boy's purpose by letting him finish a sentence.

The room falls into pointed silence.

LUKE:	I'm not Flotsam. I'm from the Ocean Commission. In Pharos.

Rowetta and Pool exchange a sharp glance.

ROWETTA: *(Casually)* Pharos, you say? You've come a mighty long way, young man.

LUKE: Aye, and it's taken me twice as long as it should have done. My boat sprung a leak and went down near Gull Point. I've been hitching lifts off tankers and fishing boats ever since.

FLUKE: I went to Pharos once, in my younger days. The streets were all a hustle and bustle, a terrible to-do, and that lighthouse! Fair hurt my neck trying to see to the top of it, and when they turned on the light it damned near blinded me!

LUKE: I need to speak with your Keeper. Do you think they'll still be up?

ROWETTA: You came in on the oil barge, didn't you? They'll still be storing the fresh barrels. The Keeper might open the door for the Ocean Commission, but whether you'd want to step inside is another matter entirely. The atmosphere's downright eerie in that place – that poor girl rattling around all on her own, with only an idiot for company.

POOL: *(Glancing at Fluke)* I know how she feels.

LUKE: Girl? I thought John Marston was the Keeper.

ROWETTA: He was. Fell to his death the winter just passed. Elle's his daughter.

LUKE: Oh.

SCENE 1

ROWETTA: It's a sorry state of affairs, and no mistake. Marston may not have been the easiest man to get along with, but he was a fine Keeper. With the best will in the world, I can't see how Elle can keep that light going – 145 especially given her difficulties.

POOL: Best she does, unless she wants to have to explain herself to an Examiner. Difficulties won't cut any ice with them, let me tell you.

FLUKE: *(Peering at Luke)* You wouldn't be an 150 Examiner, would you?

Judging by their furious expressions, this is a question Rowetta and Pool would rather he hadn't asked.

LUKE: I wish. I'm just a Junior Ship Clerk.

FLUKE: Now that is a relief, no messing nor mistaking. I've heard tales about Examiners that'd make you hair curl – men being 155 whipped like brutes with the **cat o' nine**, or thrown overboard to face the Ocean's Verdict.

LUKE: *(Stiffly)* The Commission's Sea Protocols allow Examiners the use of necessary force when dealing with pirates, wreckers or 160 **negligent** Keepers. It's vital that the seas are kept safe and the lighthouses in working order. Lives depend upon it.

ROWETTA: *(Quickly)* Quite right, young man, quite right. The seas are dangerous enough without 165 the rocks being cloaked in darkness. You won't hear a word against Examiners or the Commission in this establishment.

LUKE: Glad to hear it. *(He looks out of the window)* I might as well go up to the lighthouse now. No point drying off if I'm only going to get wet again.

ROWETTA: If you see Elle tell her Rowetta sends her regards, and there's a free drink at The Anchor for her any time she likes.

POOL: If she doesn't mind the earache caused by the constant chivvying, which is also gratis.

LUKE: I will. Good night.

Luke steels himself before stepping back out into the storm, providing another brief snapshot of the rain-lashed world beyond the inn. After the door bangs shut the remaining occupants of The Anchor share a thoughtful silence.

FLUKE: Pharos, eh?

POOL: Whatever brought him out here must be important, else he'd have turned back at Gull Point.

ROWETTA: The Wharfinger will want to know about this. Better go see him in the morning.

Pool nods.

FLUKE: I wonder what the lad wants up at the lighthouse.

ROWETTA: He wasn't about to share it with us. So it's best off we keep our mouths shut and don't give him any reason to start sticking his nose into things – like prattling on about Examiners, for instance.

SCENE 1

FLUKE: Maybe he's brought good tidings of some sort.

POOL: *(Gloomily)* Chance'd be a fine thing.

FLUKE: If you haven't got hope, what have you got? 195

ROWETTA: To have hope you have to have a future. Twenty years ago The Bluffs was three times the size it is now. How big d'you reckon it'll be twenty years from now?

POOL: Little more than the lighthouse. 200

ROWETTA: Even when this place goes underwater I'll probably still be here, bobbing about on the tide, nose pressed against the ceiling, waiting for you two to drink up!

Finishing his pint of ale with a satisfied slurp, Fluke hopefully raises the empty glass into the air.

FLUKE: Any chance of another, Rowetta? 205

The landlady sighs, defeated.

ROWETTA: Go on then. I'll join you.

She begins to pour three fresh drinks.

Scene 2

*The storm has deepened in fury, the cobblestones beneath Luke's feet streaming with rainwater as he struggles up the path to the lighthouse. As he ploughs onwards, there is a movement in an alleyway behind him, and Audrey emerges from the darkness. Despite wearing only a thin black dress and a black shawl, the teenage girl appears unruffled by the gale. When Luke looks over his shoulder Audrey melts back into the shadows. He tries to **hail** her, but his words are swallowed up by the storm.*

*Arriving at the front door of the lighthouse, Luke bangs on it several times without reply. In desperation he tries the handle, and stumbles in through the unlocked door. After the deafening rumble of the storm outside, the silence inside the lighthouse throbs with its own eerie pulse. The room is a magpie's nest of salvaged bric-a-brac: a pair of armchairs with the stuffing spilling out from their innards; a large cooking range running the length of one wall; a battered **wireless** on a table. Paintings of rolling fields and soaring mountains hang on the walls. At the back of the room a spiral staircase leads up into the lighthouse, with a guide rope pegged into the wall alongside it.*

LUKE: Hello?

There are clumsy footsteps upon the stairs, and then Sloop emerges into the living quarters. A big man with a childlike expression, he blinks owlishly at Luke.

SCENE 2

LUKE: Good evening.

SLOOP: Crosscurrents: low, deepening rapidly.

LUKE: Sorry for barging in. I was half-drowning out there. 5

SLOOP: Imminent squally showers.

LUKE: It was a bit more than a shower. *(He wrings out his sleeve for emphasis)* May I speak with the Keeper?

SLOOP: *(Impassively)* Westerly or south-westerly, 10
5 or 7. Coral: squally showers.

LUKE: I don't understand ... I thought her name was Elle. Who's Coral?

Confused by the exchange, he doesn't notice the girl appearing at the top of the staircase.

ELLE: What, not who. Coral's a shipping zone. For the weather forecast. 15

Luke jumps.

ELLE: I would have thought someone from the Ocean Commission would know that.

She pads carefully down the staircase, her hand never straying from the guide rope. Elle is a pretty girl, although her face is pale and drawn, and there are dark rings beneath her eyes. The reason for her cautious descent becomes clear as soon as she emerges into the light: her eyes are milky blanks. Elle is blind.

LUKE: How do you know I'm from the Ocean Commission?

ELLE: I may have been robbed of one sense, but I still have four left. Your voice has a trace of a Pharos accent, and there's a smell of beeswax in the air, which the Ocean Commission use to seal their documents. All their agents end up reeking of it.

As Luke stares at her in astonishment Elle bursts out laughing.

ELLE: I'm sorry. It's rude of me to tease you. The captain of the oil barge told me about you.

LUKE: Oh.

ELLE: I'm Elle Marston.

LUKE: Luke Connors.

ELLE: *(Turning to Sloop)* Sloop, there's two more barrels needing storing away in the Watch Room. Can you do that for me, please?

SLOOP: Brightening later.

ELLE: Thank you.

Elle reaches out and squeezes Sloop's hand as he shambles past her, a small act of genuine affection. Sloop continues up the steps and out of sight.

LUKE: Does he always talk like that?

ELLE: Sloop was born with water on the brain. As if this world wasn't wet enough.

LUKE: You said something about the weather forecast?

ELLE: He listens to it on the wireless every night. The voice calms him.

SCENE 2

LUKE: I see.

Elle looks up sharply, detecting a note in Luke's voice she doesn't like.

ELLE: Don't you go underestimating him. I couldn't keep the light going without him. If it weren't for the tiny minds on this island, it'd be Sloop running this lighthouse, not me.

LUKE: The tiny minds at the Ocean Commission might have a problem with that too. Sea Protocol states that the Keeper is a hereditary position, running down from parent to child. That's the way it works.

ELLE: Aye, that it is. And look where it got us. A blind girl feeling her way around a tower with ropes, like some kind of pathetic spider waiting to be washed away by the waves.

LUKE: You don't look that pathetic to me.

ELLE: Charming of you to say so. Do you mind?

*Elle reaches up to touch Luke's face. Checking his surprise, he allows her to **deftly** map the contours of his skin with her fingertips, reading his features like Braille. When she has finished she steps back thoughtfully.*

ELLE: You're younger than I thought.

LUKE: *(Proudly)* Youngest clerk in the Commission. And I'll be the youngest Examiner too, one day. Everyone on Pharos says it.

ELLE: They named it after the first ever lighthouse, you know. Pharos. It was one of the Seven Wonders of the Ancient World.

LUKE: Really? I never knew that.

ELLE: My father told me all about the Seven Wonders when I was little. They were these incredible buildings built thousands of years ago. Most of them had fallen down and crumbled away even before the floods came. There was a temple, and a giant pyramid in the desert, and the most beautiful garden you can imagine. *(She sighs)* Now there are only lighthouses.

Using the tables and chairs for guidance, Elle deftly manoeuvres herself over to an armchair and plumps herself down.

ELLE: Do you mind if we sit down? It's been a long day.

LUKE: Of course.

He takes a seat in the other armchair.

LUKE: I'm sorry for troubling you so late. I was delayed on my journey to The Bluffs and there isn't time to waste. They said you'd still be up.

ELLE: No doubt that wasn't all Rowetta said.

LUKE: *(Surprised)* How did you know I'd been to The Anchor? Was it the captain again?

Elle shakes her head.

ELLE: The smell of that place clings to a person. An aftershave of stale ale and tittle-tattle.

LUKE: Rowetta said you'd be welcome to come by and have a free drink.

SCENE 2

ELLE: *(Icily)* Did she now.

LUKE: You don't sound tempted.

ELLE: I do everything I can to stay out of that place. And you'd do the same, if you knew what was best for you.

Rain lashes against the window above the cooking range with renewed force, drawing Luke's attention towards it.

LUKE: Earlier, when I was walking up to the lighthouse … I thought I saw someone in the storm. A girl, all dressed in black.

ELLE: *(Matter-of-factly)* You wouldn't be the first person on The Bluffs to see a ghost.

LUKE: *(With an awkward laugh)* I'm afraid I don't believe in ghosts.

ELLE: That's because you've never been to The Bluffs before. This island is crowded with restless spirits and lost souls. The smaller the island gets, the closer they draw to us. *(She runs a hand down her bare arm)* I can feel them sometimes, brushing against my skin like cobwebs.

The lights flicker as the wind shrieks and writhes. For a moment the lighthouse might be the cabin of a ship, fighting to stay afloat amid the waves thundering down around it.

ELLE: So what brings you to my door in the middle of the night, Luke Connors?

LUKE: The commission sent me here to investigate a message. Sent from The Bluffs.

ELLE: What kind of message?

LUKE: A warning. It said the seas around The Bluffs weren't safe. Do you know what it meant by that?

ELLE: No ... I mean, the seas can be treacherous around the Bluffs, but everyone knows that. Sounds like a local busybody stirring up trouble, if you ask me.

LUKE: Maybe. Does anyone else live here, or is just you and Sloop?

ELLE: Just us. My mother ran away when I was a baby.

LUKE: Oh.

ELLE: *(Shrugs)* She was Flotsam. My father was a fool to think he could keep a sea-traveller tied to land. You can't hold water in a sieve.

There is a bang from outside – a door slamming in the gales somewhere. Elle stands up, apparently keen to change the subject.

ELLE: You can't go back to The Anchor in this weather. Would you like to stay here for the night?

LUKE: If it's no trouble.

ELLE: It's no trouble. If you don't mind staying in a dead man's room.

LUKE: After four months at sea, I'd just be grateful for a still floor beneath the bed.

ELLE: That, at least, I can offer you. Bring the lantern and follow me.

Luke follows her gesture to the lantern by the range and goes to collect it. Elle turns away, navigating from memory a path through the furniture to the stairs. As Luke picks up the lantern, he glances up into the window and sees Audrey staring back at him. He gasps.

ELLE: What is it? What's wrong?

Luke looks over at her, and then back at the now-empty window.

LUKE: Nothing. An old ghost. 140

Scene 3

Two years earlier. The sea, at night: the sound of giggling carries across the waves, accompanied by a loud splash of water. A small rowing boat jerks into view, carrying two occupants. In the stern sits Wanda, a bright-eyed girl, holding up a lantern. She creases up with laughter as she watches Luke struggle with the oars, digging them into the water like awkward elbows.

LUKE: *(Hissing)* Keep it down, Wanda! Someone might hear us!

WANDA: I can't help it – it's so much fun watching you. I had no idea you were so *bad* at rowing!

LUKE: I'm doing the best I can. It might help if you didn't keep rocking the boat. 5

WANDA: Pardon me for breathing.

LUKE: It wasn't my idea to come out here, you know. In the middle of the night. During a **blackout**. 10

WANDA:	*(Proudly)* I know. It was mine.
LUKE:	And like all your other bright ideas, it's crazy! When Pharos's lighthouse is on a blackout no boats can put to sea. It's the first Sea Protocol! Do you know what the Commission will do to us if a patrol boat finds us?
WANDA:	Praise our spirit of adventure?
LUKE:	*(Muttering)* I don't know why I let you talk me into stuff like this. It always ends badly.
WANDA:	You should be thanking me! Do you have any idea how boring life would be without me? How boring *you* would be?
LUKE:	Do you know how warm and asleep I'd be too?
WANDA:	That's you in a nutshell, Luke. You don't—

Wanda breaks off, peering into the darkness.

LUKE:	What is it?
WANDA:	Thought I saw a light.
LUKE:	A patrol boat? We should go back.
WANDA:	Calm down. *(Slyly)* It might not be the Commission.
LUKE:	Who else could it be?
WANDA:	Smugglers. Flotsam raiders. A ghost ship, crewed by the groaning undead …

Luke looks nervously over his shoulder as Wanda continues to scan the sea.

WANDA:	… Or just a false alarm. Relax, Luke. No sign

SCENE 3

> of any zombies, or any Commission fascists either.

LUKE: I don't know why you call them fascists. They're only trying to keep everyone safe.

WANDA: That's the problem, though! People round here are so busy trying to stay alive that they've forgotten how to actually *live*. If you're not going to enjoy yourself once in a while you might as well be dead, if you ask me.

LUKE: I've no problem enjoying myself. I just wish we could have found another way of doing it.

WANDA: Stop moaning for a second and take a look around you! *(She swings her lantern in a dramatic arc)* Look!

LUKE: I can't see anything. It's the middle of the night.

WANDA: That's the point! No ships, no lights, no people, just me and you and this boat in the entire world! Don't you get tired of Pharos – living on the same tiny bit of land, seeing the same boring faces every day?

LUKE: I guess.

WANDA: Out here, I feel ... I don't know ...

LUKE: What?

WANDA: Free.

A thoughtful look crosses her face as Luke paddles on.

WANDA: When I'm older I'm going to get a boat and head for the horizon. No maps, no plans. Just

to see what's out there. Have you heard of
Greenland?

LUKE: It's a Flotsam colony out in the middle of
nowhere. They tied a load of their **junks**
together and called it an island.

WANDA: Doesn't that sound *incredible*? Just imagine
it – a floating country!

LUKE: *(Dubiously)* The Flotsam don't acknowledge
Commission law. Anything could happen to
you out there.

WANDA: That's what makes it so exciting! You could
come with me, if you promised not to be
boring.

LUKE: To *Greenland*? Wanda, I'm applying to join
the Commission next year – what would they
say if they found out?

WANDA: *(With a sigh)* The Commission strikes again.

LUKE: What's that supposed to mean?

WANDA: Luke, I've known you since you were a baby.
You were learning Sea Protocols when
everyone else was learning their times table.
You're obsessed! I bet you had the
Commission **oath** sung to you as a lullaby,
didn't you?

LUKE: Don't be stupid.

WANDA: You did, didn't you? Come on, join in!

*The boat wobbles as Wanda stands up. Throwing
back her head she begins to sing in a merrily off-
key voice.*

WANDA: *Keep following the light!*

SCENE 3

LUKE: Shh!

WANDA: *Keep your head above the waves!*

LUKE: Wanda, the boat!

WANDA: *Order, discipline and duty!*

The boat is rocking violently now. Luke nearly drops one of the oars as he tries to drag Wanda back into a sitting position.

LUKE: I can't—! 95

WANDA: *Un—*

She stumbles, collapsing into Luke's arms.

WANDA: *(Breathily)* My hero.

LUKE: It's not funny. Can you even swim?

WANDA: Not very well, no. But since I can row significantly better than you can, I don't 100 need to.

As they disentangle themselves the waves grow larger and more insistent around them, lapping over the bow and into the boat.

LUKE: Sea's getting up. What's going on?

Raising her lantern, Wanda examines the night. A look of alarm descends upon her face.

LUKE: *(Wearily)* Wanda, if you're messing around again—

WANDA: *(Quietly)* I'm not messing around. There's a 105 ship out there. A big one.

LUKE: But there's a blackout on!

WANDA: It must have been the light I saw earlier. It's heading for Pharos harbour. Can you see it? *(She gasps)* It's a Commission ship! 110

LUKE: Impossible.

WANDA: It is! I can see its name on the bow. The *Celeste*.

Luke is trying desperately to row away from the approaching vessel, but his boat is looking smaller and smaller amid the growing waves.

LUKE: It's coming too close! The **wake** will tip us over! 115

WANDA: Oh Luke. I'm sorry.

A giant wave slams into the boat, overturning it and extinguishing the lantern. There is silence in the vast night, and then a panicked voice cries out:

LUKE: Wanda? WANDA!

Scene 4

The storm over The Bluffs has broken. Light streams in through the bedroom window, banishing the eerie shadows that had held the lighthouse in their thrall the previous night. The contented caw of gulls can be heard as they bank and wheel on the wind outside. Luke sits at John Marston's desk amidst a clutter of empty wine bottles, leafing through the Keeper's logs and charts and making notes in a small notebook.

There is a knock on the door, and Elle enters the room carrying a steaming cup of coffee. Like the

SCENE 4

lighthouse, she too appears brighter for the morning, the dark shadows and lines on her face softening in the sunlight.

ELLE: Good morning. I wasn't sure if you'd be up yet.

LUKE: *(Nods at the window)* Who needs an alarm when you've got birds?

ELLE: I suppose. I'm so used to them I don't even hear them anymore.

Luke hurries up from his desk to take the cup of coffee from her.

LUKE: Thanks.

He blows on the coffee and takes a cautious sip.

ELLE: I hope it's okay. Sloop and I don't drink coffee, and we don't tend to get many guests up here.

LUKE: It's great.

ELLE: Did you sleep well?

LUKE: Like the dead. *(He winces)* Sorry. That was thoughtless.

ELLE: It's all right. Sometimes I think lighthouses are nothing more than giant illuminated gravestones. Did you ever hear the story of Hero and Leander?

Luke shakes his head.

ELLE: Hero lived in a tower by the banks of a strait called the Hellespont. Every night her lover Leander would swim across the strait to be with her, and she would place a light in her window to guide him. One night there was a storm, and the wind blew out her light. Leander drowned. When Hero saw his body washed up on the shore, she threw herself off the tower so she could be with him in death.

LUKE: Sad story.

ELLE: You think so? They're together in the end, aren't they?

LUKE: Not in this life.

ELLE: In the next life. A better life.

LUKE: And what if there isn't another life? What about the people we've lost then? If it's all the same to you, I'll take my chances in the here and now, however long that might be.

*Elle nods thoughtfully, and feels her way over to her father's desk. When she runs her hands over the open **logbooks** her face hardens.*

ELLE: You're going through my father's things?

LUKE: His logbooks and charts. I had a couple of questions—

ELLE: *(Sharply)* You might have asked me first.

LUKE: Sorry?

ELLE: Never mind what you heard about my father, Luke Connors. He was serious about Keeping. It was more than his job – it was his life. These books were important to him. They contain details of every ship that passed The Bluffs, weather records, maintenance reports, stock **inventories**—

SCENE 4

LUKE: Shipwrecks. 50

ELLE: I suppose. What I'm trying to tell you is that they're more than just logbooks. They're personal diaries. And you're sitting there flicking through them like they're recipe books, or a little boy's notepads filled with 55 his doodles.

LUKE: Elle, your father is the reason I'm here! *He* was the one who sent the warning message to the Commission.

ELLE: My father? John Marston? 60

LUKE: Signed in his own hand. He wanted us to know that something was wrong, and he *wanted* someone to come and check his records.

ELLE: Oh. 65

LUKE: And even if he hadn't, Sea Protocol gives me the authority to read whatever lighthouse records I like.

ELLE: *(Coolly)* I see. Good to know where I stand, Junior Ship Clerk. What did you want to ask 70 me about the books?

Luke thinks about continuing the argument before deciding against it. Putting down his mug, he picks up one of the logbooks.

LUKE: Your father was incredibly meticulous about keeping his records – there are thousands of entries here, noting every last detail. But when I checked them against 75 the official records he sent to Pharos I noticed something odd. Some of the ships

25

travelling south from Lonely Shoals have been circled in his personal log, but in the official records there's no mention of them reaching The Bluffs. The *Cutty*, the *Arabella*, the *Orca* ... Do any of these names sound familiar?

ELLE: I'm afraid not.

LUKE: What about Sloop? Would he know anything about them?

ELLE: Feel free to ask him. But I'll doubt he'll understand your question, and I'm certain you won't understand his reply.

LUKE: And that's not all. Every year on April 9th, regular as clockwork, your father notes a ship passing The Bluffs. Only he doesn't name it, and there's no official record of any ship leaving a Commission port in time to get here. Or docking anywhere, for that matter.

ELLE: Well, my father never mentioned any ghost ships to me, if that's what you're asking.

LUKE: He did to me. In his note. I think that's why I'm here – to protect this ghost ship.

ELLE: Then you'd better get a move on. April 9th is two days away.

They are interrupted by a voice booming up to the bedroom from the living quarters.

BAILEY: Hello, hello? Anyone about?

Elle groans.

SCENE 4

ELLE: *(Calling out to the staircase)* We're up here, Bailey! 105

BAILEY: Capital, capital!

The tramp of footsteps upon the stairs signals Bailey's ascent. He is lecturing someone loudly on lighthouse architecture as he climbs.

LUKE: Who's Bailey?

ELLE: The Wharfinger. The most powerful man on The Bluffs. And the most self-important.

Bailey bustles grandly into the bedroom. On an island where the inhabitants have lean physiques hewn by hard work, he is flabby and rotund. A metal chain covered in rust hangs proudly around his neck. Bailey's wife Sophie follows in his wake. Sophie is half the Wharfinger's age, a beautiful woman who looks ill at ease in his company – a glittering gemstone locked in a glass display case.

BAILEY: Come, come, my dear. Let us not keep our young Keeper waiting! *(He turns to Elle without waiting for his wife to reply)* And how does this bright and sunny day find you? 110

ELLE: Busy.

BAILEY: The burden of public office. I understand completely. 115

There is a pause as he waits expectantly to be introduced to Luke.

ELLE: *(Relenting)* Wharfinger, this is Luke Connors. He's from the Ocean Commission.

BAILEY:	Yes, my dear girl, I know all about our esteemed visitor. I'm only sorry I wasn't warned about your arrival, else I could have prepared a more fitting welcoming.
LUKE:	The Commission thought a low-key arrival was best in the circumstances.
BAILEY:	And who am I to question the wisdom of that august institution? Might I be permitted to inquire as to the purpose of your visit?
LUKE:	Nothing special. Just a regulation check-up on the lighthouse.
BAILEY:	Well I have no doubt you will be impressed by the operation here. When Elle's poor father died we might have worried about who was taking over – such a young girl! And one with her own particular daily challenges to face. But face them she does!
ELLE:	*(Dryly)* You're too kind, Bailey.
BAILEY:	*(Regally)* Praise where praise is due.

Sophie has made no effort to join the conversation, her gaze fixed on the view out of the window. Now she coughs, and tugs at the high collar of her dress.

LUKE:	Are you OK?
SOPHIE:	I'm fine, thank you. A bit short of breath, perhaps. Would you mind if I opened the window?
ELLE:	Be my guest.
LUKE:	Let me—
SOPHIE:	*(Quickly)* I can do it. *(She smiles)* But thank you.

Sophie walks over to the window, moving all but one of the empty wine bottles off the sill as she opens it. She closes her eyes as a breeze floats in, and takes a deep breath of air.

BAILEY: Like all truly precious things, a winter flower or a crystal glass, my wife is fragile and must be treated with great care. Isn't that right, my love?

His wife ignores him, but the Wharfinger doesn't seem to mind. He returns his attentions to Luke.

BAILEY: I trust you'll enjoy your stay here, Luke. The Bluffs is a tight-knit community, but a welcoming one. The rising water and the draining sands of time only serve to bring us closer together. *(Touching the chain around his neck)* It's like my Wharfinger's chain. The metal may be rusted and coated in brine but the links still hold.

LUKE: Can't be easy, living so far away from other islands. I've been told to take care on the ocean here.

BAILEY: Wise words. The seas around The Bluffs demand respect. There are crosscurrents and sandbanks, and more than one way to end up on the rocks. And not every ship is **helmed** in the manner you'd hope: inexperienced sailors, dry-soles who've barely stepped aboard a boat; drunk, criminal or plain careless Flotsam captains; pirates. Elle can light the path and point out the dangers, but if men are too stupid or **feckless** to heed her advice …

He shrugs.

ELLE: Speaking of which, I believe the Commission have some questions about some ships—

LUKE: No they don't.

He gives Elle a sharp look that is entirely wasted on her.

ELLE: My apologies. It seems I was mistaken.

BAILEY: No matter, no matter. *(Shaking Luke's hand)* If you need anything, my boy – absolutely anything – my office can be found at the heart of the **wharf**.

SOPHIE: *(Quietly)* It was nice meeting you.

LUKE: You too.

*The couple leave the bedroom together. Bailey's voice continues to echo up from the staircase until the slam of the front door **heralds** his exit.*

ELLE: I thought you wanted to find out about those ships? Or am I the only person you want to cross-examine?

LUKE: You're the only person I trust enough to ask. I don't want Bailey finding out why I'm here. Not yet.

ELLE: That's the first sensible thing you've said this morning. Bailey knows every bit of shady business that goes on here. If something *is* wrong on The Bluffs, you can bet he's involved.

LUKE: I didn't get the feeling his wife liked him all that much.

SCENE 4

ELLE: *(Snorts)* Sophie can't stand Bailey. He **lured** her into marrying him by promising to take her away before The Bluffs disappears completely. That was ten years ago, and she still hasn't set foot off the island.

LUKE: Why doesn't she leave him?

ELLE: Who knows? Her parents died of flood disease when she was young. Bailey's the only person who's ever taken care of her. Maybe she doesn't know where to go. You'd have to ask Sophie – I barely know her. She was my mother's closest friend, but after my mother disappeared Sophie stopped coming to the lighthouse.

LUKE: She came today.

ELLE: On Bailey's insistence, I'd imagine. He always wheels her out when he's trying to impress.

LUKE: Maybe.

ELLE: *(Archly)* You have another theory? Do you think Sophie was desperate to meet you – the handsome young man from Pharos, here on Ocean Commission business? It is very impressive, when you think about it. *(She pretends to fan herself)* I'm quite overwhelmed.

LUKE: Very funny. I'm just saying, she was acting strangely. It's not *that* warm in here, and yet she made a big show out of opening the window.

ELLE: You heard Bailey. She's as fragile as a crystal flower, or whatever it was.

Luke walks over to the window and picks up the sole remaining bottle on the sill. He holds it up to the light, frowning, and then removes a small piece of paper that has been slipped inside the neck.

ELLE: What is it? 225

LUKE: Sophie left a message. For me. *(He reads it thoughtfully)* A message in a bottle.

Scene 5

*The sea wall that encircles The Bluffs is a castle **rampart** battered by years of siege. An exposed pathway with a railing looks out over a concrete wall sloping down to the sea, where the water gnaws hungrily at its base. The fierce wind coming in off the ocean flings spray over the seaweed-strewn pathway.*

Sophie stands waiting by the rail, her gaze trained on a distant spot far out to sea. Wrapped in thought, she doesn't flinch when a large wave crashes against the sea wall. The spray falls away to reveal Audrey on the path behind her. Audrey is about Elle's age, a decade or so younger than the Wharfinger's wife. Dressed all in black, she is a vague, otherworldly shadow in the daylight.

AUDREY: Waiting for someone?

Sophie whirls around.

SOPHIE: Who are you?

AUDREY: Audrey's the name; come down from Greenland.

SOPHIE: Then if you've any sense you'll get back on your boat and go back there. There's no love on this island for Flotsam.

AUDREY: Aye, we're all beggars and thieves to you, aren't we? Not every Flotsam walks round with fistfuls of charmed seaweed and a greedy eye upon your purse, you know.

SOPHIE: *(Quietly)* I know that.

AUDREY: Maybe that's why I'm here. Heard you were friend to the Flotsam, once.

SOPHIE: Once. But she disappeared a long time ago.

AUDREY: That's Flotsam for you. Whether it's a Commission courtroom or the bottom of the ocean, there's no happy ending for me or my **kin**.

SOPHIE: We'll all be heading to the bottom of the ocean soon enough, Audrey. If it's sympathy you're after, I've none to spare.

AUDREY: *(Scornfully)* Sympathy. What use is that?

SOPHIE: Then what *do* you want?

AUDREY: I'm guessing you've never seen Greenland? It's a beautiful place – a hundred junks lashed together to make a living, creaking island. Flotsam drift in from across the ocean, sailing alongside for a time before drifting away again. We never settle in one place for long. Either the wanderlust takes us, the Commission moves us on, or the money dries up and we have to look for work. That's why my brothers Billy and Rogan left Greenland for Lonely Shoals.

	They signed up for a ship bound for Pharos called the *Cutty*. Only the *Cutty* never reached Pharos. It sank in the waters off The Bluffs.
SOPHIE:	That's horrible – I'm so sorry.
AUDREY:	*(Nods)* So that's why I'm here. My mam's sick with grief, and someone needs to find out what happened.
SOPHIE:	What happened? Audrey, it's a tragedy but the *Cutty* wouldn't be the first vessel to go down near the Bluffs. These are—
AUDREY:	… dangerous waters. Aye, so everyone keeps telling me. But there's talk among the Flotsam – whispers upon the waves, echoes in seashells – that it's more than that. That nature is being given a helping hand.
SOPHIE:	What do you mean, a helping hand? Are you talking about wreckers?
AUDREY:	I'm talking about murderers, plain and simple.
SOPHIE:	Audrey, that's absurd!
AUDREY:	*(Firmly)* And don't think it's just the Flotsam who smell a rat. This morning I saw a light out at sea, almost as bright as the sun.
SOPHIE:	You can't be serious. There hasn't been a Light Vessel in these parts since my grandfather's time.
AUDREY:	I know what I saw.
SOPHIE:	Why are you telling me all this? It's got nothing to do with me!
AUDREY:	Maybe not, but I'll wager your husband's got blood on his hands.

SCENE 5

SOPHIE: *(Angrily)* Take it up with Bailey, then! I don't want anything to do with this.

AUDREY: Too busy feeling sorry for yourself, eh?

SOPHIE: *(Pushing her away)* I've heard enough of your wild accusations. Leave me alone! 70

AUDREY: Maybe you were once a friend to Flotsam, but you're friend no more. Who cares if one of ours is murdered, or two – we're nothing more than thieves and frauds, aren't we? 75 Well if it's charmed seaweed you're after—

As she kneels down to scoop up a handful of seaweed from the path, Luke appears on the horizon, his hair ruffled by the wind.

AUDREY: —it's charmed seaweed you'll get!

She hurls the seaweed into Sophie's face, who recoils as though slapped.

LUKE: Hey!

As he runs over Audrey slinks away down the path, flashing a look of hatred back at Sophie before disappearing into the wind.

LUKE: Are you all right?

Sophie scrapes the wet strands of seaweed from her face and clothes, disgust etched on her face.

SOPHIE: I'm ... I'm OK. 80

LUKE: Who was that?

SOPHIE: A Flotsam girl called Audrey. She's a troublemaker, nothing more.

LUKE: I saw her last night, in the storm. I wasn't sure she was real. 85

SOPHIE: Oh, she's real all right. Unfortunately, so is this seaweed.

She catches Luke's eye as he pulls a stray strand of seaweed from her hair, and almost breaks into a smile. Pulling a tissue from her handbag, Sophie dries off her face.

SOPHIE: I'm glad you found my note. Sorry for the secrecy – there are some things I don't want Bailey to hear. Or Elle, for that matter. 90

LUKE: *(Confessing)* Elle was there when I read it. I asked her to come with me but she said no. She … she said she didn't care what you had to say.

SOPHIE: Elle's a regular hermit crab, and it's a tough shell she's wrapped herself in. Though God knows she's had to be strong, what with a lighthouse to run and her mother gone and her father the way he was … 95

LUKE: I've heard he was a difficult man. 100

SOPHIE: *(Darkly)* John Marston was a monster, a violent, bitter drunk. The Bluffs breathed a sigh of relief when he died. He always had a temper on him, but after Marina disappeared something became **unmoored** in his mind. 105

LUKE: Marina – was that Elle's mother? She told me she ran away.

*Sophie snorts with **derision**, and turns away to look out over the sea.*

SCENE 5

LUKE: Sophie? What is it?

SOPHIE: I shouldn't blame her. How can she see without eyes? 110

LUKE: Are you talking about Elle?

SOPHIE: I know what people say: Marina was Flotsam; she was always going to return to the sea. But I swear to you that – for whatever reason – she loved that man with all her heart, 115 and she would never have given up him *or* Elle. The night Marina vanished I went to the lighthouse to see her. I could hear Marston yelling from the path, and when he answered the door he was shaking with rage. He tried 120 to push me away but I wouldn't budge until I'd seen Marina. Eventually she appeared, her eyes wet with tears. Marina told me not to worry and that she'd see me the next day. It was the last I saw of her. John Marston saw 125 to that.

LUKE: *(Shocked)* You think the Keeper killed his wife?

SOPHIE: I'm absolutely certain of it. Did Elle not tell you that he jumped from the tower on the 130 anniversary of Marina's disappearance? Everyone thought it was sorrow that did for him, but not me. It was guilt.

LUKE: What about Marina's body? If Marston killed her what happened to it? 135

Sophie laughs humourlessly.

SOPHIE: Have you not learned about the currents that surround The Bluffs? Whole ships can sink

	and leave no trace – how could anyone hope to find the body of one poor girl?	
LUKE:	But if there's no body, and Elle's father's dead …	140
SOPHIE:	Aye, there's no one left to tell the truth. More's the pity.	

*Luke brushes the hair from his eyes, a **dubious** look on his face.*

SOPHIE:	You don't believe me.	
LUKE:	It's not like that. It just all sounds a bit … dramatic.	145
SOPHIE:	I get it. We're just a bunch of silly islanders, slowly drowning out here in the middle of nowhere. Well you just wait, Mr Ocean Commission.	150
LUKE:	What do you mean?	
SOPHIE:	Your arrival has made people nervous. Pool came down to the wharf at first light to see Bailey and they were a long time talking.	
LUKE:	I met Pool in The Anchor.	155
SOPHIE:	That's no surprise. It might be Pool who opens his mouth, but it's Rowetta's words that come out. Mark my words, she and Bailey are plotting something.	
LUKE:	They can plot all they want. They wouldn't dare harm a member of the Ocean Commission.	160
SOPHIE:	If you think that you don't know how desperate people here really are. *(Urgently)* You have to listen to me, Luke. Unless you	165

SCENE 5

	want to end up like Marina, you need to forget about The Bluffs and take the first boat back to Pharos. And take me with you.
LUKE:	What?
SOPHIE:	I have to leave this island. My husband. This life.
LUKE:	Sophie, Sea Protocol states that I can't interfere in personal matters when I'm on Commission business. My hands are tied.
SOPHIE:	This place has shrunk so small I can barely breathe. People constantly watching every move I make.
LUKE:	Sounds like a goldfish bowl.
SOPHIE:	I should be so lucky. Goldfish don't remember anything. In The Bluffs, you can't forget a thing.

170

175

180

She turns back to the railings and leans upon them, gazing out to sea.

SOPHIE:	Audrey said she saw a light out on the ocean. In the daylight.
LUKE:	Really? She thinks an Examiner's out there?
SOPHIE:	Like I said, she's a troublemaker—
LUKE:	*(Abruptly)* I have to tell Elle. She needs to know.
SOPHIE:	*(Pointedly)* Really? And does Sea Protocol state that you're to warn Keepers if an inspection is on the horizon?

185

190

She reaches out and grabs him as he turns to leave.

SOPHIE: Wait. Truly, I don't know what Bailey's up to but he's meeting Rowetta at The Anchor tonight. You might want to stop by.

LUKE: Thanks. I will do.

As Sophie watches him hurry away along the seawall she notices another strand of seaweed stuck to her blouse. With a sigh she tosses it back into the sea and watches the waves devour it.

Scene 6

*The Anchor is busy, shadows blown away like cobwebs by brightly burning oil lamps. Raucous knots of Crewmembers nudge and shove one another as they swap jokes and tall tales, while a fiddler and a guitarist brew a heady sea shanty in the corner of the room. A tall Stranger in a long coat stands waiting at the bar between Pool and Fluke, who are **moored** to their usual stools. By contrast Rowetta is a bustling blur of industry – breaking off from serving drinks, she darts out from the bar to collect glasses from a nearby table.*

STRANGER: Another here, please!

ROWETTA: *(With a glare)* And I'll be with you presently, sir, but as you can see I currently have my hands full. Unless I grow a third arm or my long-lost twin appears you may have to wait. 5

She returns to the bar with an armful of glasses, rolling her eyes at Pool and Fluke, who snigger obediently. She puts down the glasses and begins to pour the Stranger's drink.

SCENE 6

ROWETTA: Tide drag me under, but we have a crowd in tonight.

POOL: The *Haiti* docked here this afternoon. Stopping off for supplies on its way to Gull Point. Explains all the strangers.

ROWETTA: Yes, thank you Pool. I had noticed the huge great ship by the wharf. Is Bailey not here yet?

POOL: Nope.

ROWETTA: Typical. That man's never here when you actually need him.

She hands the freshly poured drink to the Stranger, who pushes some coins across the counter and takes a deep swig.

STRANGER: Funny little island, this.

ROWETTA: If you say so.

STRANGER: Sure, it's just a shrinking scrap of land now, little more than a rocky bald head, but imagine what it must have been like before the floods. It would have been a mountaintop lost in clouds! The people below would have had to crane their necks just to see it, shielding their eyes from the sun. There's no telling what secrets are buried beneath us now – a volcano's mouth, a president's head, the remains of a wooden ship …

Fluke peers down at the floor, as though looking for clues. He frowns.

FLUKE: A wooden ship?

POOL: He means the Ark, stupid. Came to rest on a mountaintop, didn't it?

Fluke stares at him.

POOL: You know: 'Two by two, the animals went on'?

FLUKE: Oh, I see. *That* flood.

POOL: If there is a God upstairs, he is nothing if not consistent.

FLUKE: Where's our Noah, then?

ROWETTA: Even he would think twice afore letting you two on board. Unless he's missing a pair of fishwives.

FLUKE: Wonder if there were any mermaids on the Ark. *(To the Stranger)* Did I ever tell you the tale of the time I fell in love with one?

POOL: Please God, not again.

FLUKE: Like a dream she was, a damp hand around my heart. When she kissed me she left a salty tingle on my lips that lasted until the morning after.

STRANGER: Sounds like quite a woman.

FLUKE: You have no idea.

The Stranger nods politely and leaves the bar, joining some of the Crewmembers at their table. Pool studies him through narrowed eyes.

POOL: What's his game? All that talk of secrets makes me nervous.

ROWETTA: You ask me, we've a few too many unfamiliar faces on the island at present. Some Flotsam girl's been talking nonsense about missing

SCENE 6

>   ships, and now that lad from the Ocean
>   Commission's turned up to stick his nose in.
> FLUKE: He was talking to the Wharfinger's wife
>   down on the sea wall, asking questions.
> POOL: He oughta be careful, asking questions. He
>   might end up getting an answer he doesn't
>   like.
> ROWETTA: Speak of the devil.
>
> *They break off as the door to The Anchor opens and Elle and Luke enter the pub.*
>
> ROWETTA: Well look'ee here. Two more to come aboard
>   our humble Ark – this time it's a pair of
>   doting lovebirds.
> POOL: *(Darkly)* More like **mayflies**, if they don't
>   watch out.
>
> *He flinches as Rowetta leans over and clips him around the ear. Elle's arm is linked though Luke's for support, and he leads her carefully to the table the landlady has just cleared. As they take a seat Rowetta bustles over, elbowing Pool in the side as she passes the bar.*
>
> ROWETTA: Good evening, my young friends! A delight
>   to see you here. I trust the lighthouse is still
>   shining brightly in your absence?
> ELLE: Sloop can take care of things for an hour or so.
> POOL: You left the halfwit in charge?
> ELLE: He's not a halfwit.
> ROWETTA: *(To Pool)* You keep your trap shut. It's half a
>   wit more than you can boast.

She turns back to Elle with a bright smile on her face.

ROWETTA: What can I get you both?

ELLE: Just a glass of water for me.

LUKE: And me.

ROWETTA: I can see you're planning on quite the evening. Two glasses of water it is.

As Rowetta stomps back behind the bar Elle pulls her shawl closer around her, a look of distinct unease on her face.

LUKE: Are you all right?

ELLE: *(Snaps)* For God's sake, Luke, I'm fine!

LUKE: Sorry I asked.

They sit in moody silence as Rowetta returns from the bar with two cloudy glasses of water.

ROWETTA: *(Ironically)* On the house.

Receiving no reaction, she leaves them to it. Luke sips from his water, looking around the pub. Finally Elle speaks.

ELLE: *(Hesitantly)* It's the smell of this place – like a waterlogged graveyard, filled with bloated corpses. When I was younger there were times I'd have to come here to find my father. He'd be sat at the bar with Pool and Fluke, drinking. Sometimes he'd be pleased to see me, sometimes he wouldn't. Sometimes he'd shout at me and tell me to go to Hell. But the smell was always the same.

SCENE 6

At this moment Bailey bustles inside The Anchor, looking visibly flustered. He ignores Sophie, who follows several paces behind and is careful to avoid looking over at Luke's table.

ROWETTA: Wharfinger! How nice of you to join us!

BAILEY: I've no time for your tongue. 95

ROWETTA: What is it?

As Bailey leans over the bar to speak to her, in the background the Stranger stands up and clinks his glass with the other Crewmembers.

STRANGER: Three cheers for the *Haiti*! Hip hip!

CREWMEMBERS: Hooray!

BAILEY: *(Conspiratorially)* One of my men found a ship moored out at sea. It was painted 100 bright red, with a large light fixed into a tower.

ROWETTA: A Light Vessel? You mean there's an Examiner in these waters?

BAILEY: Closer to home than that. The Light Vessel 105 was empty. He must have come ashore with the *Haiti*!

STRANGER: Three cheers to all the ships that pass through these waters!

ROWETTA: *(In a disbelieving hiss)* He's on the island? 110

STRANGER: To the *Orca*!

CREWMEMBERS: Hooray!

Bailey's face turns to stone. Rowetta and Pool freeze.

STRANGER:	To the *Arabella*!	
CREWMEMBERS:	Hooray!	
ROWETTA:	Pipe down, or you'll be out on your ear.	115

Luke looks on curiously as Bailey tries to shush the Stranger.

STRANGER:	To the *Cutty*!	

Picking up on the strained atmosphere, the Crewmembers do not cheer this time. The musicians stop playing as Bailey elbows his way over to the Stranger.

BAILEY:	Listen here, what's all this about? Who are you?	
STRANGER:	No one.	
FLUKE:	Everybody's someone.	120
STRANGER:	I have no name. I am not a person. I am a word.	
BAILEY:	Whatever are you talking about?	
STRANGER:	I am a word, and that word is truth. I bring light into a world of darkness.	125
ROWETTA:	Bailey, *he's* the Examiner!	

The crowd stifles a gasp. The Crewmembers shuffle backward and even Pool and Fluke look impressed. The Examiner takes another sip from his drink, completely unfazed.

EXAMINER:	Present.	
BAILEY:	And what brings you to The Bluffs?	
EXAMINER:	Dark currents. Ghost ships.	
BAILEY:	I'm not sure I understand.	130

SCENE 6

EXAMINER: I'd wager you do.

BAILEY: Naturally, anything we can do to help an honoured Examiner—

EXAMINER: Save your crawling. You'll get your knees wet.

*Luke whispers something in Elle's ear, then rises from his table and **interjects** himself between the Examiner and Bailey.*

EXAMINER: What can I do for you, lad? 135

LUKE: The name's Luke Connors. I'm a Ship Clerk at the Ocean Commission.

The Examiner bursts out laughing.

EXAMINER: Of course you are! When I was your age I wanted to be Pharos's Head Keeper. But this is adult business – nothing to concern you. 140

LUKE: You can check my warrant, if you like.

He produces a sealed parchment from his pocket, but the Examiner waves it away.

EXAMINER: That might mean something back on Pharos, but the sea doesn't care about pieces of paper.

LUKE: *(Shocked)* But Sea Protocol states that— 145

EXAMINER: *(Derisorily)* Sea Protocol! Move aside, lad.

LUKE: No!

The Examiner pushes back his long coat, revealing a wicked-looking whip hanging from his belt.

EXAMINER: *(Deliberately)* You're a very small boat in the middle of a very large storm, Ship Clerk. If I

	were you, I'd head for port before something bad happens.	150
FLUKE:	Hey, hey, hey! The seas may be rough but this island's a gentle cove. Take a deep breath and a step back, Examiner – the boy means no offence.	155

Before anyone can blink the Examiner's whip darts across the room like a snake's tongue, smashing Fluke's glass and sending everyone by the bar ducking for cover. The fisherman howls with pain, clutching his hand.

ROWETTA: Hey! Stop that!

EXAMINER: For impeding Commission business, he's lucky not to feel the cat's claws across his back. And unless you want the same I'd keep your mouth shut. 160

A shocked silence falls over the inn. As Fluke gingerly examines his hand, the Examiner returns his whip to his belt and addresses the inn in a powerful voice.

EXAMINER: Listen up! Until my investigation is finished no one is to put to sea without my express permission. Understood? Wouldn't want anyone to suffer the same fate as the *Cutty* now, would we? 165

He turns to Elle, whose expression remains defiant.

EXAMINER: Unless there's another blind girl on this island, I'm guessing you're the Keeper.

ELLE: You'd be guessing right.

EXAMINER: Well then, Keeper. Would you be so kind as to accompany me to the lighthouse? 170

ELLE: As you wish.

As the Examiner escorts Elle towards the door, with Luke in close attendance, Rowetta produces a mop and begins sweeping up the shattered glass and spilt beer. She turns and glares at the two musicians in the corner of the room.

ROWETTA: And what are you two waiting for? I haven't paid good money for a pair of silent songbirds, too busy gawping to open their beaks. Come on! 175

The musicians hurriedly pick up their instruments and begin to play, noise returning to The Anchor as the stunned onlookers resume their conversations.

POOL: *(Gloomily)* And the band played on.

Scene 7

*Five months earlier. Luke is hard at work behind a desk in a tiny clerk's office, against a vast blue backdrop of ocean maps pinned to the wall. Strains of music and the murmur of a vast crowd float up from the street below, through the window where Ripley, the Senior Ship Clerk, maintains a **disconsolate** watch. He shakes his head.*

RIPLEY: *(Bitterly)* And a happy Pharos Day to you too. May all your ships spring a leak. And the seas be cold and choppy.

Luke doesn't look up.

RIPLEY: I'll wager we're the only people on the whole damned island working. I had planned to spend the day watching the **flotilla** parade with a sweet young miss from the **Dry Dock**. But instead I have to spend the day with you.

LUKE: *(Not listening)* Mmm.

RIPLEY: I see you're unmoved by the unfairness of this situation. Wouldn't you rather be outside too? Don't you have a special someone you'd like to spend Pharos Day with?

LUKE: *(Quietly)* Not any more.

RIPLEY: Lost your friend during a blackout, didn't you? There's too much cause for mourning in this world. Take my advice: make the most of being alive while you can. The clock's ticking.

*Breaking away from the window, he picks up one of the **ledgers** from Luke's desk.*

RIPLEY: I mean, look at this stuff! 'Cape Hook Lighthouse, October 30th: sighting of Flotsam junk *Ariel* off the east coast. Doubtful that they have any trading papers. Request Examiner investigation.' Could it not have waited until tomorrow?

LUKE: Not if they want to catch the *Ariel*.

SCENE 7

RIPLEY: By the time we get word to Cape Hook that ship will have long since vanished into the sea mist.

LUKE: Doesn't mean we can't try. Rules are rules.

RIPLEY: *(Sourly)* Quite the company man. No wonder they let you join so young. You've probably got the Commission oath tattooed on your chest, haven't you?

LUKE: I know the words, if that's what you mean.

RIPLEY: Chapter and verse, no doubt.

LUKE: Someone's got to be in charge, or the seas would be full of pirates. The strong would be free to pick on the weak. Sea Protocols are there to protect people. Just because the waters are rising it doesn't mean that we just give up.

RIPLEY: You sound just like an Examiner.

LUKE: That's nothing to be ashamed of.

RIPLEY: *(Mockingly)* Of course not! The briny knights of the Ocean Commission, guiding their Light Vessels to the furthest reaches of the ocean to keep the seas safe and the lighthouses in good working order!

LUKE: You make it sound like a bad thing. When people don't follow the rules they get hurt. I could never get Wanda to see that.

RIPLEY: I'm all for safe seas, Luke. I'm just not convinced that letting a bunch of power-drunk **vigilantes** loose on the ocean is necessarily the best way to achieve it.

LUKE: If they didn't have power and authority who would listen to them?

RIPLEY: Let me tell you a story. Centuries before the flood there was an ancient king who had his subjects carry him down to the beach on his throne. They put him down at the water's edge where he held up his hand and commanded the tide to stop. It didn't, of course, and all he got for his troubles was a pair of wet feet.

LUKE: That's what you get for being stupid.

RIPLEY: Stupid? On the contrary. This king was a wise old **coot** who thought his subjects should see that even kings have limits to their power. Something you might do well to think about. No one is infallible, Luke. If you have blind faith in these people, you're asking to be disappointed.

LUKE: If you don't care about Examiners or the Commission why did you join it?

RIPLEY: Who said I don't care about the Commission? I just don't always like the way it works, that's all.

*Ripley sighs and turns back to the window. Opening a fresh ledger, Luke discovers a folded note **secreted** within its weathered pages. He reads it, frowning.*

RIPLEY: *(Curiously)* What've you got there?

LUKE: Some kind of note. It was tucked into one of the Keeper's Reports.

SCENE 7

RIPLEY: A love letter from a distant island maid, perhaps?

LUKE: Not exactly. It says *'The seas aren't safe. Can no longer protect the ghost.'*

RIPLEY: Where's it from?

LUKE: *(Checking the ledger)* Er ... The Bluffs.

RIPLEY: *(Snorts)* That'll be John Marston, then. You can take that with a pinch of salt, lad. Rumour has it Marston likes to hit the bottle.

Luke gets up and examines the map on the wall behind him for The Bluffs, tracing his finger across the blue until he finally locates the island in the top left corner.

LUKE: It's a far way out.

RIPLEY: Beyond the boundaries of known civilization. The people out there are little better than Flotsam. There's Lonely Shoals beyond them and that's about it ...

He breaks off.

RIPLEY: Damn.

LUKE: What is it?

RIPLEY: Read me the note back again.

LUKE: *'The seas aren't safe. Can no longer protect the ghost.'*

RIPLEY: *'The ghost'*? He can't mean ...

LUKE: Ripley, what's going on?

Ripley doesn't answer, murmuring to himself as he studies the map.

RIPLEY: If Marston's right the Commission will *have* to send someone to The Bluffs. *(He groans loudly)* It'll be me, won't it? Two months shivering on a boat to the middle of nowhere! I'm cursed, I tell you.

LUKE: I'll go.

RIPLEY: Hmm?

LUKE: Send me to The Bluffs. I'll find out whether there's anything suspicious going on there.

RIPLEY: *(Doubtfully)* I don't know, lad… You really think you're ready for this?

LUKE: Try me.

A loud cheer goes up from the crowds outside. Ripley glances towards the window, chewing on his lip.

RIPLEY: *(Eventually)* We'll need clearance from the Commission.

LUKE: Of course.

RIPLEY: But you'll convince them you're up to it, won't you lad? An enthusiastic believer like you. A quick blast of company oath might not go amiss.

A grave smile playing on his lips, Luke stands up and places his right hand over his heart.

LUKE: Keep following the light,
Keep your head above the waves,
Order, discipline and duty …

RIPLEY: … Until the last light fades.

LUKE: *(Solemnly)* Until the last light fades.

Scene 8

In the lighthouse living quarters, Sloop sits in an armchair with his eyes closed and a peaceful smile upon his lips. The wireless is on, filling the room with a comforting crackle of static, like an open fire. A smooth voice is reading out the weather forecast.

FORECASTER: Mudlark: Rough, occasionally rough, high. Poor visibility.

The front door bangs open, sending Sloop springing from his armchair in fright. The Examiner strides inside the lighthouse, his hand gripped firmly around Elle's arm. Luke follows closely behind them, protesting loudly.

LUKE: … let go of her!

EXAMINER: I'm just making sure the girl doesn't fall over. Wouldn't want her losing her way in the darkness.

SLOOP: *(Frightened)* Rough!

ELLE: It's all right, Sloop. I'm fine. *(Acidly, to the Examiner)* I can take it from here, thank you.

EXAMINER: As you wish.

She snatches her arm away, rubbing the bare flesh where the man's hand has held her.

FORECASTER: Aquamarine: Low, 987, deepening rapidly.

SLOOP: Deepening!

He shrinks back as the Examiner strides over to him, until their faces are only inches apart. Sloop wilts under the inspection, sinking down to the floor and hugging the table bearing the wireless.

EXAMINER: What's wrong with him?

ELLE: There's nothing wrong with him! Leave him alone!

EXAMINER: I didn't touch him. If a man can't stand to be looked at it suggests to me a guilty conscience.

ELLE: He's nothing to feel guilty about. Without him I could never keep the lighthouse running.

EXAMINER: No, you wouldn't, would you? Given your handicap, I'm guessing he's the one responsible for keeping the light clean.

ELLE: *(Firmly)* Every inch of every lens, every day. Without fail.

The Examiner looks back at Sloop, who remains cowering by the wireless.

EXAMINER: Very reassuring.

A burst of static erupts from the wireless, and then the Forecaster's voice echoes around the living quarters, in a more urgent tone than previously.

FORECASTER: We have word coming in of an urgent storm warning for The Bluffs in the next twenty-four hours. Repeat, Storm 10, The Bluffs.

EXAMINER: Well now. It would seem our task just got a little more urgent. Wouldn't want any ships going down in the storm, would we?

LUKE: You're talking about the ghost.

SCENE 8

EXAMINER: I don't know what you mean. 35

LUKE: Yes you do. And so did John Marston – that's why he mentioned it in his warning. He was talking about a ship. A secret ship, that passes The Bluffs on April 9th every year.

EXAMINER: Perhaps your soles aren't bone-dry after all. Aye, there's a ship passing by tomorrow night. 40

LUKE: Why all this secrecy? What's the ship's cargo? Gold?

EXAMINER: In a manner of speaking. 45

LUKE: Why can't I find it in the official records? Where does it set sail from?

EXAMINER: Greenland, of course.

LUKE: But that's impossible! Commission ships are forbidden to deal with the Flotsam! 50

EXAMINER: Why do you think they keep it a secret?

LUKE: What does it carry?

EXAMINER: Flotsam workers. The Commission may say that they're all criminals and **outlaws** but it always needs extra hands to work at the Dry Dock off Pharos – and Flotsam are always willing to pitch in if the money's right. The Commission don't want people to know so the ship docks at Pharos in the dead of night, during the lighthouse blackout. 55 60

LUKE: *(urgently)* Blackout? What's the name of this ship?

EXAMINER: The *Celeste*.

Luke stares at the man, dumbfounded.

ELLE: Luke? What is it?

LUKE: *(Hoarsely)* It's a ghost ship, all right. We've got to make sure it passes The Bluffs safely. Enough lives have been lost already.

EXAMINER: Now you're talking some sense. So how about you stop interfering and let me do my job? You can turn that wireless off for a start.

With the forecast at an end, all that remains is dull static. Luke switches off the wireless and helps Sloop to his feet.

ELLLE: What about the other ships you mentioned back in The Anchor? The *Cutty*, and the rest? They're the same ones Luke asked me about.

EXAMINER: Let's just say I'm here to make sure the *Celeste* doesn't suffer the same fate.

LUKE: Really? You think they might try and target it?

ELLE: Who's they? Target what? What are you talking about?

LUKE: *(Reluctantly)* I think a group of wreckers has been operating on The Bluffs, and I think your father was one of them. That's why he circled those ships in his personal log, and left them out of the official records.

ELLE: *(Bitterly)* You do, do you? And what exactly would you know about my father?

LUKE: I know he sat down and wrote the world a warning about this island before he killed himself.

SCENE 8

ELLE: Then you can go to hell, do you hear me? You *and* your precious Ocean Commission.

LUKE: Elle, please—

Elle turns away.

EXAMINER: As enlightening as this has been, it's high time we headed up to the Lantern Room. I need to examine the light.

ELLE: Be my guest. We've never failed an examination before.

EXAMINER: You haven't been examined by me yet.

ELLE: Stay down here, Sloop.

EXAMINER: Ah ah ah – not so fast. He'll stay where I can see him. I've only your word that he's a fool. *(Beckoning to Sloop)* Come with me.

The small party troops up the staircase, with Elle leading the way, her hand upon the guide rope, and the Examiner bringing up the rear. They emerge at the top of the lighthouse in the Lantern Room, a bell-shaped room completely encased in glass. The light sits dormant in the centre of the room, a complex honeycomb of lenses. Through the glass a perilously exposed walkway is visible encircling the Lantern Room, while beyond the setting sun has turned the horizon a deep burgundy.

LUKE: Some view.

ELLE: People always used to tell my father that. He'd laugh in their faces. Spend a day watching the sea, he'd tell them, on your own, without a soul for company. Spend a week. Spend a year. Lighthouses are built on the edge of the world, on cliff faces and rocky outcrops, deserted beaches. Day after day they're battered by winds and spray and storms, the ground beneath their feet being eaten away, inch by inch. *(With a humourless laugh)* They say a strain of madness runs through Keeping families – is it any surprise?

With great ceremony the Examiner produces a spotless white cloth from his pocket and unfolds it.

EXAMINER: If light is truth then even the smallest shadow is a lie, an affront. I'm going to wipe this cloth down every inch of lens, and for every black speck or grimy smear that appears on it, the Keeper's going to pay with a lash from the cat o' nine across her back.

LUKE: *(Incredulously)* What?

EXAMINER: A mark for a mark.

LUKE: That's insane! Sea Protocol states that a Keeper can be punished for **gross negligence** or criminal behaviour, but you can't whip them over a speck of dirt!

EXAMINER: I can do what I please, so long as the lighthouses keep shining while they're here. A mark for a mark, remember?

The others watch on helplessly as the Examiner kneels down and wipes one of the light's lenses. When he inspects the cloth, a smile breaks out across his lips. He shows the cloth to Luke, pointing at a black mark on the material.

EXAMINER: That's one.

SLOOP: *(Mumbling)* Rising winds.

The Examiner ignores him, wiping down the next lens and checking the cloth once more. Luke goes pale when he shows him the cloth.

EXAMINER: Two and three. The cat will be busy tonight.

SLOOP: Threat of gales.

EXAMINER: *(Snaps)* Hold your tongue, or you'll feel the lash harder than the Keeper!

SLOOP: *(Shouting)* Storm Warning! Storm Warning!

ELLE: Sloop, no!

With a roar Sloop charges forward, knocking Elle to the ground as he crashes into the Examiner, sending him sprawling across the floor of the Lantern Room. Sloop tears the cloth from the other man's hands, stamping on it as though it were on fire. Luke races over to help Elle back to her feet.

ELLE: Run, Sloop!

Sloop blinks, uncomprehending. Luke is forced to shove him towards the stairs – finally Sloop gets the hint, clattering away down the steps. The Examiner staggers to his feet and makes to give chase, only to find Luke stood in his way.

EXAMINER: What in the dead seas do you think you're doing? That madman attacked an officer of the Commission!

LUKE: That 'madman' was terrified out of his wits. He thought you were going to hurt Elle.

EXAMINER:	I have the right to check the lights. No one can question my authority.	
LUKE:	You've lost your mind. And I'll say as much to the Commission.	

The Examiner's eyes narrow.

EXAMINER:	You really thinks they'd take your word over mine, dry-soles?	150
LUKE:	Let's find out, shall we?	
EXAMINER:	We're a long way from Pharos, boy. The only court I pay heed to is the ocean, and my cat o' nine is the gavel.	155

He unhooks the whip from his belt and grabs Elle. She bites her tongue to prevent herself from crying out.

LUKE:	Don't hurt her!	
EXAMINER:	One way or another justice will be done. Either you face the Ocean's Verdict, or the Keeper gets the cat's tongue right here.	
LUKE:	No! Okay, leave her alone and I'll come with you.	160
ELLE:	Are you crazy? Luke, you'll drown!	
EXAMINER:	Only if he's guilty.	
LUKE:	I'll do whatever you want. Just please, let her go.	165

He breathes a sigh of relief as the Examiner pushes Elle to one side and points the cat o' nine at Luke.

EXAMINER:	Let's make haste. A storm's brewing.

ELLE: I'm coming with you!

LUKE: You can't. You have to make sure the lighthouse is working when the *Celeste* passes by tomorrow night. It *has* to make it through to Pharos, Elle. More lives than mine are relying on it. 170

ELLE: What about you?

LUKE: Don't worry about me. I'll be fine.

She reaches out to touch him but the Examiner intervenes, grabbing Luke by the collar and marching him down the stairs, leaving Elle alone in the Lantern Room.

EXAMINER: I'll see justice done, though the heavens may open and the seas erupt! 175

Scene 9

The deck of Pool's dredger pitches and heaves amid towering waves, water pouring in over the sides of the boat and washing across the wooden decking. Night has fallen, and the sea is dark save for a dazzling distant beacon: The Bluffs' lighthouse. Rowetta and Bailey are clinging to the rail on the dredger's deck. The pub landlady looks glum, the Wharfinger downright miserable.

ROWETTA: Wind's picking up. Won't be long 'til the storm hits.

BAILEY: This is madness. Utter madness!

ROWETTA: Why don't you go below decks and tell his Royal Lightness, then? This voyage wasn't my idea. 5

BAILEY:	If the Examiner wants to test the boy and drown himself in the bargain then that's his own affair, but he's no right dragging us down with him!	10
ROWETTA:	A point that could have been more usefully made back on dry land when – I couldn't fail to notice – you were quieter than a church mouse.	
BAILEY:	There's no use arguing with a lunatic.	15

*Rowetta makes a **contemptuous** noise, before launching into a mocking impersonation of her **pompous** companion.*

ROWETTA:	You need a boat, Lord Examiner? Why not take Pool's dredger? Witnesses? We'd be honoured to accompany you!	
BAILEY:	*(Darkly)* If you ask me, it's the girl who's behind this.	20
ROWETTA:	You need carrying down to the wharf, Lord Examiner? If I get down on my hands and knees you can ride me. Yes, like a pig, with my rusty chain for a rein!	
BAILEY:	*(Ignoring her)* She pretends not to see anything but she knows what she's doing, all right.	25
ROWETTA:	Are you talking about Elle? Bailey, you can't be serious.	
BAILEY:	Then how come she's safe and warm in the lighthouse and we're all out here, then? And how come, out of all the people on The Bluffs, the Examiner chose me, you and Pool for witnesses? Just a coincidence, hmm?	30

ROWETTA: When it comes to this kind of thing, I'm a great believer in the power of plain old bad luck.

The Examiner appears on deck, one hand on his cat o' nine whip, the other on Luke's arm. He looks up into the night sky, his eyes shining with triumph.

EXAMINER: A stormy courtroom, fit for a traitor! Dark galleries hunger for a verdict.

BAILEY: Examiner, the weather is getting worse by the second. We have to turn back!

EXAMINER: You would make justice wait upon your convenience?

BAILEY: I would not condemn us all to the same sentence.

EXAMINER: Screw your courage to the sticking place, Wharfinger. The sea sends only the guilty down. Innocent men have nothing to fear.

Rain comes slanting down across the dredger's deck, accompanied by a howling wind.

LUKE: I've done nothing wrong. They're the wreckers, not me!

BAILEY: An outrageous lie! He'll say anything to save his own skin.

LUKE: Tell me I'm wrong! I've figured out how it worked. You and Marston arranged which ships to sink, and he'd turn off the light. When the ships hit the rocks, Pool used his dredger to go through the wreckage. *(To*

	Rowetta) I'm guessing you were responsible for selling what you found. Everyone who lands on The Bluffs ends up at The Anchor at some stage, don't they?
BAILEY:	I've never heard such nonsense. The boy's brine drunk!
EXAMINER:	Maybe he is and maybe he isn't. Truths can tumble from even liars' mouths. I waited to try the boy 'til the *Celeste* was nearly upon us so I could be sure the three of you could pose it no threat. This whole island's rotten to the core. I've half a mind to make you all face the Ocean's Verdict.
POOL:	Then maybe we should get on with it.

*The dredgerman has appeared in the cabin's doorway, dressed in a yellow **sou'wester**. Of all the people aboard the boat, his voice is even and calm.*

EXAMINER:	Shouldn't you be at the **helm**?
POOL:	I've dropped anchor. You asked for witnesses, didn't you?
LUKE:	Don't you see, Examiner? They want me dead because they know I'm telling the truth!
EXAMINER:	And their turn will come, but it's you we're here to try. *(To Pool)* A hand here, man!

Pool walks over and grabs Luke's other arm. In the grip of two bigger and stronger men, Luke is powerless to prevent himself from being dragged to the side of the boat and pressed back over the railing.

SCENE 9

EXAMINER: Let the waves decide! How do you find the **defendant**? 80

Without warning Pool releases Luke's arm and dives on the Examiner, ripping the cat o' nine from his hands. Surprised, the Examiner stumbles backwards into the railing, whereupon Pool drives his shoulder into the other man's chest. With a chilling scream the Examiner topples over the railing and into the sea, where he is swallowed up by the black waves. Pool watches the man drown with calm satisfaction.

POOL: Guilty.

LUKE: *(Gasps)* You killed him!

POOL: Rather it were you?

BAILEY: What were you thinking, man?

POOL: You heard him. We would have been next over the rail. 85

BAILEY: But we would never have touched the *Celeste* – Marston always insisted on it! And now you've killed an Examiner! If the Commission ever hears about this ... 90

POOL: *(Firmly)* But they won't, will they? Not if we tie up all the loose ends.

Luke is suddenly aware that the other three are staring at him.

LUKE: You can't keep going on like this. How many more people are going to die to keep your secret? 95

POOL: Just one.

ROWETTA: You don't understand, Luke. We're drowning out here – day by day, inch by inch. When you lose hope you lose everything. You change. 100

LUKE: That doesn't give you the right to sink ships. It doesn't give you the right to *kill* people—

He stops and stares.

ROWETTA: What is it?

He points over her shoulder.

LUKE: The lighthouse! Look!

As one they turn and look. The distant sky is an unbroken black canvas. The light from the lighthouse has winked out.

POOL: That damned girl! I knew we should never have left her there alone. 105

LUKE: Elle'd never let the light go out. Something's wrong. We have to go back to the lighthouse!

ROWETTA: The lad's right. Pull the anchor up and take this tub back to harbour. 110

POOL: Hang on.

ROWETTA: Pool?

POOL: Let's think about this for a minute.

ROWETTA: Pool, this isn't the time. We have to get back to The Bluffs! 115

BAILEY: No, this needs sorting now. There's been a lot of talk about wrecking, and we don't need any such foolish chatter reaching dry land.

SCENE 9

POOL: And there's a dead Examiner to explain, too. Don't think I'll be taking the blame for that.   120

ROWETTA: *(Desperately)* The boy's right. Hasn't there been enough killing?

BAILEY: Keep out of it, woman.   125

ROWETTA: You've got a nerve, Wharfinger. Now the Examiner's gone you've rediscovered your bottle!

POOL: Time for talking is over. We've come this far.

He cracks the cat o' nine against the deck and advances on Luke, who scans the deck in vain for a weapon. He manages to duck out of the way when Pool cracks the whip again, only to slip on the wet decking. At that moment a wave slams into the dredger, engulfing Luke and sweeping him overboard.

LUKE: Aargh!   130

ROWETTA: Luke!

She rushes to the side of the dredger and scans the sea, resisting Pool's attempts to drag her away.

BAILEY: Come away from there, fool woman!

ROWETTA: You can't just let him drown!

POOL: You want to go in after him, be my guest! But I'm taking the boat back to port.   135

He turns and hurries back inside the cabin, Bailey following close behind him. As the anchor rattles up from the seabed and the boat's motor growls into life, Rowetta is left alone on deck, staring helplessly out over the waves.

Scene 10

The lighthouse is shrouded in darkness, the living quarters a jungle of threatening silhouettes. Rain lashes down hard against the windowpane, backed by the wild shriek of the wind. For a few seconds nothing stirs inside the building, and then a nervous voice floats down from the top of the stairs.

ELLE: Hello?

She moves carefully down the staircase towards the living quarters, her footfalls echoing on the metal steps.

ELLE: Is anyone there?

Unusually for the Keeper, fear is evident in her voice. There is no reply from the darkness.

ELLE: Sloop? Is that you? The generator's shut down and I can't get it working again. I think someone's tampered with it.

As she nears the bottom of the stairs Elle missteps, tumbling on to the floor with a loud cry of pain. She picks herself up slowly, rubbing her knee.

ELLE: *(In a harder voice)* There's no use pretending you're not here. I can smell The Anchor on your clothes. Tell me who you are.

Buried in the darkness, someone is sitting very still in one of the armchairs.

FLUKE: Did I ever tell you about the time I fell in love with a mermaid?

SCENE 10

Elle's hand flies to her breast in relief. Fluke leans forward and opens the cover of a gas lamp on the table in front of him, illuminating his face in a soft orange glow.

ELLE: Fluke! You scared the life out of me! What are you doing here?

FLUKE: *(Wistfully)* She was the most beautiful creature in the world, with dark eyes like the midnight ocean. She looked a little like you, no denying or **gainsaying**. I first caught sight of her when I was out fishing. I was a young man back then, with barely a hair on my chin or a thought in my head. She was lying out on the rocks by the water's edge, basking in the sunshine. I was so enchanted I ran my boat aground on a sandbank. I can still hear her laughter, like raindrops on the morning tide.

ELLE: What are you talking about?

FLUKE: *(Sharply)* I'm talking about *love*, you stupid little girl.

Elle takes a step backwards. In the distance, there is the faint call of a ship's horn.

FLUKE: I thought I had caught my true love – but had I known what was going to happen, I would have tossed her back into the sea. It turned out that I was the one caught up in a net, a treacherous web with threads woven from lies and deceit. She smiled at me but she gave her heart to another – a cold, cruel man. I was left with nothing, saddled with a sea cow of a wife while the sound of the mermaid's laughter rang in my ears.

ELLE: *(In a small voice)* Are you talking about my mother?

FLUKE: A Flotsam mermaid, a creature half of land, and half of sea. I told Marina that she'd made a mistake choosing Marston but she wouldn't listen to me, confusing old Fluke for a green-eyed monster. Then one night I came a' stumbling and a' rolling out of The Anchor and I saw her hurrying through the streets, her face streaked with tears like the rain. Your father had been cruel to her again. I offered to help her but she laughed at me and pushed me away. She *laughed* at me. Like I was a child, or no man at all.

Elle's hand flies to her mouth.

ELLE: It was you. You killed her.

FLUKE: I was trying to help her. But she wouldn't stop laughing at me!

Fluke buries his face in his hands, sobbing loudly. Elle retreats to the range, her hands scrabbling the sideboard for an implement, a weapon – anything to protect her. The ship's horn sounds again, louder than before.

ELLE: *(Desperately)* Did you hear that, Fluke? The *Celeste* is approaching The Bluffs. You have to help me turn the light back on!

When Fluke looks up at her his eyes are wet with tears, but his face is wreathed in a murderous smile.

FLUKE: Now why would I want to do a thing like that?

ELLE: You were the one who shut down the generator. You *want* the *Celeste* to hit the rocks!

FLUKE: I'll shed no more tears nor say no more sorrys for lost Flotsam life, that's for sure. And it won't be me who gets the blame, neither. I'm not the wrecker on this island.

ELLE: You're talking about killing hundreds of innocent people!

FLUKE: I'll not have a Marston preach to me on the matter of wrecking. Your father was happy to turn off the light, if Bailey told him. They used to sit there in The Anchor – Bailey, Marston, Rowetta and Pool – plotting and planning and divvying up the spoils. They thought old Fluke was too much of a fish brain to let him in on the action but I knew what was going on. I've known about the ghost ship passing on April 9th for years – I've just been waiting for the right time to act.

ELLE: Don't you care about innocent people dying?

FLUKE: I died on a rainy night fifteen years ago. Tonight it's the *Celeste*'s turn. And yours.

Reaching down by the side of the armchair, he produces a curved fisherman's hook. He runs the metal point across the table, making a horrible scraping noise on the wood that makes Elle shudder with revulsion.

ELLE: Keep away from me …

FLUKE: I've reeled in tougher catches than a little
blind girl. Come here! 85

Elle screams as Fluke lunges forward with a snarl. She makes for the spiral staircase, grabbing on to the guide rope and scrambling up the stairs. Fluke chuckles and follows after her – he is in no hurry.

FLUKE: Now where are you off to? Once you taste the metal of my hook, you'll stop wriggling soon enough.

Elle appears in the gloom of the Lantern Room, panting frantically. She stumbles, falling against the light. Out to sea the Celeste's horn gives out another blast. Fluke tops the staircase. He is out-of-breath, but visibly enjoying the chase.

FLUKE: Nowhere left to hide, little fishy.

He stands over Elle, raising his hook aloft.

AUDREY: Fluke! 90

The sound of his name stops Fluke in his tracks. He looks up to see Audrey standing on the exposed walkway running around the outside of the Lantern Room. Wrapped only in a black cloak, she appears unmoved by the storm raging around her.

FLUKE: Who's there?
AUDREY: A vengeful ghost.

Fluke pales.

FLUKE: It can't be.

AUDREY: *(In a ringing cry)* Murderer!

FLUKE: *(Disbelievingly)* Marina? 95

The light bursts into dazzling life, its beam aimed straight at the fisherman. Fluke howls with pain, dropping his fishhook as he clutches at his eyes.

FLUKE: I can't see!

Audrey advances through the revolving beam of light to the glass doorway that connects the walkway to the Lantern Room.

AUDREY: Murderer and a coward, whose vicious heart could not stand rejection. Mark my words, I'll see you swap the ocean's depths for a fiery pit of Hell! 100

With a hoarse yell the blinded Fluke charges at Audrey, his hands reaching out for her throat. As the beam of light continues to revolve, the two of them are sunk into darkness – there is a chilling scream, and when the light returns only Audrey remains standing on the walkway.

ELLE: What's happening? Who's there?

Audrey enters the Lantern Room and crouches down beside Elle, placing a comforting hand on her shoulder.

AUDREY: Hush now. Fluke fell off the tower. Nobody will hurt you now.

ELLE: Who are you?

AUDREY: I told Fluke. A wrathful spirit. And there's 105 more blood to spill before I can rest. *(Glances towards the stairs)* Sounds like the front door – I'd best be gone.

ELLE: No, wait!

Audrey vanishes down the stairs. Several seconds elapse, and then Elle shrinks back at the sound of footsteps upon the stairs. Luke bursts into the Lantern Room, crying out with relief at the sight of her.

LUKE: Elle! Are you all right?

ELLE: Luke!

Luke's clothes are wet through, and he staggers over and hugs Elle with the weariness of someone who has expended every last drop of energy.

ELLE: You're wet through! And so cold!

LUKE: And tireder than I've ever been, but I'm alive.

ELLE: *(Faltering)* When the Examiner took you away I thought … I thought I was never going to see you again. But you came back to me.

LUKE: Always.

The pair slump to the floor in each other's arms, the light periodically bathing them in bright white. For the third time the Celeste's horn sounds – a triumphant exclamation of the ship's safe passage.

LUKE: The *Celeste*!

ELLE: The light came on in time. It's safe. We're all safe.

Scene 11

Daybreak. The wind has dropped and the rain has eased, and there is a hint of sunshine behind the grey clouds. Gulls call out to one another as they arc and swoop through the sky. Luke and Elle stand together at the sea wall, leaning against the railing. Below them the water laps contentedly against the concrete.

LUKE: Are you OK?

ELLE: *(Smiling)* For the hundredth time, I'm fine! I should be the one worrying about *you*.

LUKE: I'm just happy to be on dry land.

ELLE: I can't stop thinking about you swimming back from the dredger. It's a miracle you didn't drown.

LUKE: It was such a strange thing. Even though it was pitch black and the sea was all around me, I never doubted where I was going. It was as if the lighthouse was still shining, bright as day.

ELLE: Stronger than Leander.

LUKE: I told you I wasn't willing to wait until the next life.

He softly takes her hand in his. Tentatively Elle draws closer, laying her head against his shoulder. She reaches up and touches his face with her fingertips, mapping it carefully.

LUKE: Forgotten what I look like?

ELLE: I never forget a face. Especially yours.

*They share a few seconds' silence, listening to the splash of the waves and the gulls' **caws**.*

ELLE: I suppose you'll be heading back to Pharos soon.

LUKE: When word gets out that an Examiner's gone missing all hell's going to break loose. Sea Protocol states that I have to return to Commission in person and make a statement.

ELLE: Ah. I should have guessed. Sea Protocol.

LUKE: And then there's the small matter of the wreckers ...

ELLE: I heard that Bailey and Pool took off on the dredger in the middle of the night. Apparently Rowetta's back behind the bar of The Anchor, pretending nothing has happened.

LUKE: She can pretend all she wants. When word gets out what she's been up to, she'll be alone in that inn for the rest of her life. No one will want to share their table with a wrecker.

ELLE: Audrey seems to have vanished into thin air. I wanted to say thank you. If it hadn't been for her ...

LUKE: I don't understand how she could have got off The Bluffs. Only one vessel's left the island since last night, and that was Pool's dredger.

ELLE: She said she had unfinished business. Fluke may have killed Marina but he wasn't

SCENE 11

            responsible for the death of Audrey's brothers. Maybe there's your answer.

LUKE: Really? You think she ...?

ELLE: I've no idea. But if I were Bailey or Pool I'd keep one eye over my shoulder.

She shivers, and pulls herself closer to Luke.

ELLE: It's going to be strange when everything goes back to normal. Very quiet.

LUKE: You could always come with me, you know. When I leave.

ELLE: Are you joking? I can't just hop on a boat and set sail! What about the lighthouse?

LUKE: Find Sloop and let him take care of it. Like you said, he's more than capable.

ELLE: But the Keeper's a hereditary post! What would the Ocean Commission say?

LUKE: I'm guessing they'd be furious. But then The Bluffs is very far away from Pharos, and what they don't know won't hurt them. How long will The Bluffs be here, anyway?

ELLE: You've changed your tune. I thought all you cared about was rules and regulations.

She's teasing him, but the delight in her voice is unmistakable.

LUKE: Rules and regulations are important. I'm not sure they're *all* I care about, though.

He squeezes her hand. As the sun breaks through the cloud, in the distance two figures appear on the path behind them: Sophie and Sloop.

LUKE:	We've got company.	70
SLOOP:	*(Excitedly)* High winds!	
ELLE:	Sloop!	

He lumbers over to Elle and gives her a fierce hug.

ELLE:	Where have you been? I've been so worried about you!	
SOPHIE:	I found him hiding in a warehouse down by the wharf. The poor man was shaking with fear. I thought it'd be best if we came and found you.	75
ELLE:	Thank you.	
SOPHIE:	Don't mention it. You should see The Bluffs this morning! Everyone is out on the streets, talking and gossiping. I don't know whether they're horrified or secretly excited.	80
ELLE:	*(Ruefully)* Glad we could provide them with a bit of drama.	85
SOPHIE:	Everyone knew that Bailey and his cronies were up to something but Fluke – a murderer? I still can't believe it. I thought he was just a harmless old man.	
ELLE:	Even shallow waters can hold hidden dangers.	90
SOPHIE:	I suppose. I feel as though I owe you an apology. All these years, I had thought your father—	
ELLE:	*(Firmly)* My father made his own reputation. The most important thing is that my mother reclaims hers. She went to her grave still true to her family.	95

SCENE 11

SOPHIE: Don't worry. I'll make sure people know the truth about Marina. 100

LUKE: You're planning on staying around? With Bailey out of the picture I'd have thought you'd have been on the first boat out of here.

SOPHIE: I know. But with him gone The Bluffs 105 doesn't feel as small as it did yesterday. I don't know how much time we've got left until the water claims us but in the meantime the people here deserve better. Maybe there's a chance to improve things. 110

LUKE: *(Thoughtfully)* Hold on. With Bailey gone, you're next in line to succeed him.

SOPHIE: Me? Wharfinger? Are you sure?

LUKE: *(Grins)* Sea Protocol.

SOPHIE: I don't know … 115

ELLE: Of course you do. You could start at the same time as Sloop.

LUKE: You're coming with me?

ELLE: What do you say, Sloop? Think you'll be all right running the lighthouse without me 120 getting in the way?

SLOOP: Visibility good.

LUKE: That settles it, then. The first thing you and Sophie can do is get a message to Ship Clerk Ripley at the Ocean Commission. Tell him 125 what happened here. Tell him he was right about the Examiners.

ELLE: Wouldn't it be better if you did that?

LUKE: We will. Eventually.

Elle gives him a curious look.

ELLE: What are you saying? 130

LUKE: I thought first we might get a boat and head for the horizon. No maps, no plans. Just to see what's out there.

ELLE: That doesn't sound like the Luke Connors I know. 135

LUKE: Maybe not. But there's an old friend of mine who I think would approve. She always said there was no point in being alive if you weren't going to live, and now I think I understand what she 140 meant. What do you say?

When Elle nods he picks her up and spins her around.

ELLE: *(Laughing)* Have you even got a boat? How are we going to get around? Back to hitching lifts off oil tankers?

LUKE: There's an empty Light Vessel moored out 145 to sea, remember? I figure its owner won't have any more use for it.

ELLE: Really? We could take it?

LUKE: I don't see why not. We are on official Ocean Commission business, after all. 150

There is a blast from a ship's horn far out to sea.

ELLE: Did you hear that? A ship!

A smile breaks across her face as the others turn and watch the ship passing safely by The Bluffs, their hands protecting their eyes from the sun.

SLOOP: Sunny spells, brightening later.

The End

Glossary

benevolent kind
blackout no lighting at all
brine salt water
cat o' nine nine whips knotted together
caws a harsh cry
conspiratorially plotting together
contemptuous scornful
coot a water bird
defendant person accused of something
deftly skillfully
derision mockery
disconsolate unhappy
dry dock where boats are mended
dubious doubtful
feckless irresponsible
flotilla several boats sailing together
gainsaying denying
goading annoying
gross negligence not caring *at all*
hail (someone) call
helm where you steer the ship
helmed steered by a person
heralds announces
inquisitive curious
interjects interrupts
inventories lists of things
jibes taunts
junks a type of boat
kin family and relations
ledgers books of lists – usually money
listing here, moving to one side
logbook an official record of where a ship sails
lured tempted

mayflies small delicate insects that live on average for only one day
moored when a boat is tied up to land
negligent not caring
oath a promise
outlaws criminals
pompous self-important
rampart a wall to keep out the enemy
secreted hidden
sentinel guard
sluicing washing/running down
sou'wester a water and windproof coat
supping drinking
turbulent disordered, violent, not calm
unmoored not tied up to land
vigilantes people who have their own laws
wake a strong movement of water
wharf where ships unload
wireless a radio

Activities

Activity 1: Introducing character

After reading Scene 1

> In this activity, you will look at how the scene is set as the play opens. You will also examine mythologies mentioned in the play.

1. **Work on your own.** Look at the opening stage directions. They are dramatic and detailed. Pick out the words you are unfamiliar with and write them (and an explanation of their meaning) on a table like this one.

Description	Meaning
turbulent (page 1)	Disordered, violent, not calm.
sentinel (page 1)	A soldier or guard, someone who keeps watch.

2. **Work on your own.** Read the opening scene of the play again. Then draw and label a detailed picture of it. Check to make sure you have the island correctly laid out. You may choose to use colour to add to the impressions we get of it.

3. **Work with a partner.** Asking questions is what is called an 'active reading strategy'. It helps you to understand the text. List all the questions you have at the end of Scene 1.

4. **Work on your own.** Write a paragraph to show what you have learned about the environment in which the characters live. Include how they feel about 'Keepers' and 'Examiners'?

ACTIVITIES

Activity 2: Leaving clues

After reading Scene 2

> In this activity, you will examine how the writer leaves clues and information about characters through their background and environment.

1. **Work on your own.** Imagine you are in the lighthouse for the first time, like Luke. Make a list of what you can see, hear, smell, touch and taste. Try to think of a minimum of two things for each sense. What are your first impressions of the lighthouse as a place to live?

2. **Work on your own.** We learn a great deal about Elle in this scene. Create a character profile sheet that includes all the information we know about her, her situation and her parents.

3. **Work on your own.** This scene uses many similes and metaphors: Elle, for example, describes herself as being *like some kind of pathetic spider* (line 55, page 13). Write down as many similes and metaphors as you can from this scene. Then write a short description of a stormy night, which includes similes, metaphors and personification.

4. **Work with a partner.** Imagine that Luke writes a record of each day for his report. What would it contain at the end of this day? Remember to include his journey to The Anchor, his meeting with Rowetta and the others, and what he thinks of Elle and The Bluffs.

Activity 3: Thinking and feeling

After reading Scene 3

> In this activity, you will explore how characters might feel or think about each other.

1. **Work on your own.** Make notes on:

    - how Luke feels about Wanda
    - what Wanda thinks about Luke
    - how Luke might feel at the end of the scene
    - who you think is to blame for what happens.

2. **Work in a group of three or four.** Create a role-play where one of you is Luke and another is Wanda. The other one or two students will voice the thoughts inside the characters' heads that they keep hidden from one another. For example, Wanda could actually feel very frustrated with how Luke sticks to rules. Perhaps he starts to think that she is right?

3. **Work on your own.** Rewrite this scene as a chapter from a novel. Remember to use detailed description and to create an atmosphere of building tension. It could be written in the first or third person.

4. **Work in a group of three or four.** Discuss what you think happened next to Wanda and the impact that it may have had on Luke.

ACTIVITIES

Activity 4: Understanding characters

After reading Scene 4

> In this activity, you will explore what we learn about characters as they are introduced to us.

1 **Work on your own.** We are introduced to the character of Sophie in this scene. Write at least five sentences that explain what we learn about her and her situation.

2 **Work on your own.** Imagine that you are Sophie and have written the message in the bottle that Luke finds. What does it say? Write a 300-word message. Try to use clues from the play to make your note believable.

3 **Work in a small group.** A soliloquy is where an actor speaks directly to the audience, revealing their inner-most feelings. Write the soliloquy Sophie might deliver about her thoughts and feelings. Use Scene 4 for the content of her speech. Remember, you must convey the feelings you think she may have from the clues given in this scene.

Activity 5: Reading between the lines

After reading Scene 5

> In this activity, you will use clues and read between the lines.

1. **Work on your own.** We learn in this scene that *there's no love on this island for Flotsam* (lines 6–7, page 33). List six other things we learn about the Flotsam community and their way of life. Why do you think the people of The Bluffs dislike them so much?

2. **Work on your own.** In plays, a key method used by writers to give the audience information about characters is through dialogue. In this scene we have two main conversations. In the first, Audrey talks to Sophie and we learn about Audrey. In the second, Sophie talks with Luke and we learn about Sophie. Create spider diagrams to show what we learn in each conversation about each character.

3. **Work in a group of three or four.** There are fewer stage directions in this scene than most others. Decide what stage directions you would give to the characters to tell them how to speak, what their body language should be, how they should look at each other and what their facial expressions should be.

4. **Work in the same group of three or four.** Re-enact the scene and evaluate how effective your directions were. One person should act as observer.

Activity 6: Getting to know you

After reading Scene 6

> In this activity, you will focus on how characters are developed and how a writer builds a picture of a character for the audience.

1 **Work on your own.** The Examiner is gradually introduced, starting with a stage direction then becoming more central to the scene through his words and actions. List the occasions when he says or does something and what the impact is. Choose at least five quotations to show what you mean. For example, *a tall Stranger in a long coat stands waiting* (stage instruction, page 40) implies he is mysterious but we don't know at this point if he is a threat.

2 **Work with a partner.** Imagine that Bailey and Rowetta meet for a drink after hours to discuss what has happened. Produce a new scene in the form of a script that shows what they are worried about and what they are thinking. Stick to their characters.

3 **Work in a small group.** Discuss your impressions so far of Rowetta, Bailey and Elle. What one question would you like to ask each person and why?

Activity 7: Using information

After reading Scene 7

> In this activity, you will collect information from the text that supports the opinions you have formed about the characters.

1 **Work on your own.** Luke believes in *order, discipline and duty* (line 126, page 54). Find four things he says in this scene that support this opinion of him as someone who follows the rules. Think back to previous scenes, how true do we know this to be?

2 **Work on your own.** Ripley is a pessimist. He can be negative and sarcastic. How do the stage directions show he is not an optimist? Find four examples of his dialogue that support this view. Now create two spider diagrams. The first should show the synonyms for PESSIMISTIC for Ripley; the second should show the synonyms for OPTIMISTIC for Luke.

3 **Work with a partner.** King Canute was an English King who tried to turn back the tides. Find out everything you can about him to create an information booklet. Remember to include when he lived, what life was like at that time, and what opinions there have been of him and his actions.

4 **Work on your own.** This is a story of mysteries and secrets. So far the writer has given us lots of half pieces of information, lots of clues and hints at things to come. Imagine that you are a detective on the case. Write up your notes so far on 'The Case of the Ghost Ship and the Bluffs'. Include what you have discovered, what you have been told and, at this point, what you might think will be the outcomes.

Activity 8: Story structure

After reading Scene 8

> In this activity, you will look at the structure of the play.

1 **Work on your own.** Stories usually have four basic sections:

   Section 1, Set-up: The opening situation is established.

   Section 2, Conflict: A problem happens and becomes increasingly worse.

   Section 3, Climax: The problem at its most serious.

   Section 4, Resolution: The problem is resolved.

   Using these sections, you can re-tell entire stories in only four sentences. Choose some well-known stories and have a go.

2 **Work on your own.** Scene 8 is part of the *conflict* phase of the play. The Examiner arrives and things become dramatically worse. Explain how this is. Who is under threat because of the Examiner's arrival? Remember that there are different characters involved in various threads of the story at this point.

3 **Work on your own.** Plan the *set-up* and *conflict* for a mystery or a ghost story of your own. Do not plan the whole story.

4 **Work with a partner.** Plan several possible climaxes and resolutions for each of your stories. Then decide which you think is the best. Write the story in full.

Activity 9: Sentence structures

After reading Scene 9

> In this activity, you will look at how writers aim to convey information to the audience.

1 **Work on your own.** This scene is where Luke explains what has happened and what has been covered up. Important things are revealed. When a character explains things out loud to another character this is called 'exposition'. In your own words explain the roles of Rowetta, Bailey, Poole and Elle's father, what has been happening on The Bluffs and what the 'Ghost Ship' really was.

2 **Work on your own.** Imagine that you are Bailey and you are back at The Anchor. How will you explain the disappearance of the Examiner and Luke? Write the speech you will give. Remember to write in character – Bailey is arrogant and pompous, so this should come across.

3 **Work with a partner.** Re-draft each other's speeches. Perform your speeches in front of each other or to the whole class. Then critically evaluate each other's performance and add commentary. Was the speech effective? Was the speaker convincing? What could you change?

Activity 10: Seen on screen

After reading Scene 10

> In this activity, you will learn how fiction can be presented through film.

1. **Work on your own.** Re-read Scene 10. Make a list of the key moments. Then look at this list of camera angles.

Very Wide Shot	VWS	Subject only just visible.
Wide Shot	WS	Subject takes up the full frame.
Mid Shot	MS	From the knees or waist up.
Close Up	CU	Head and shoulders or just face.
Extreme Close up	ECU	Extreme detail
Cut in	CI	Shows some (other) part of the subject in detail.
Cut Away	CA	A shot of something other than the subject.
Over Shoulder Shot	OSS	Looking from behind a person at subject.
Point of View	POV	View from the subject's perspective.
Aerial shot	AS	Looking down on events.

2. **Work with a partner.** If this scene were in a film, what camera angles from the list above would you use? Write a few sentences about each choice.

3. **Work with a partner.** Create a storyboard showing how you would film this scene. Beneath each frame include details of the camera angle, music, sounds, special effects and any dialogue.

Activity 11: Tying up loose ends

After reading Scene 11

> In this activity, you will look at the resolution and effectiveness of the ending of the play.

1. **Work on your own.** The ending of the a play is called the 'resolution'. This means that all the loose ends are tied up. (Usually, the 'goodies' are rewarded and the 'baddies' are punished.) Discuss how the stories of Elle, Luke, Sophie, Marina and Audrey are resolved in this final scene. Write a paragraph for each one.

2. **Work on your own.** Do you think the final scene is a good ending? Is it satisfying? Write a letter to the author, Tom Becker, explaining what you think and giving suggestions for how he could have improved, amended or changed it.

3. **Work in a group.** Discuss what alternative (different) endings the play could have had. What might some of the outcomes have been? How do you think things could end differently for Elle's father? Her mother? What about Audrey?

Activity 12: Making movies

After reading the play

1. **Work in a group.** Imagine that this play is being made into a Hollywood blockbuster and you are in charge of casting. Knowing what you do about the characters, which actors would you cast to play them and why? Come to an agreed cast list, then write a short blurb for the film.

2. **Work on your own.** From your discussions create a short storyboard trailer. This should have six key scenes in pictures and six short captions beneath each one. The aim is to summarize the play and entice the audience.

3. **Work on your own.** What if some things in the play hadn't happened? For example, what if Audrey had **not** been in the lighthouse when Elle was attacked? Pick out five key moments and write two alternative outcomes/courses of actions. (You could create spider diagrams if you prefer.)

4. **Work in pairs.** Research the mythology surrounding the underwater world of Atlantis. Create a presentation to give to the class.

5. **Work on your own.** The ending of a play is usually called the 'resolution'. This is where all the loose ends are tied up and the plot falls into place. Explain how the stories of Luke, Elle, Sophie, Marina and the 'Ghost Ship' are tied up here. Do you find this a satisfactory ending to the play? What could the author have done differently?